Praying the Bible

Praying the Bible

An Introduction to *Lectio Divina*

by

Mariano Magrassi, O.S.B.

Translated by

Edward Hagman, O.F.M. Cap.

A Liturgical Press Book

THE LITURGICAL PRESS
Collegeville, Minnesota

Cover design by Ann Blattner. Illustration: Book of Hours, ca. 15th century, *Pentecost,* Hill Monastic Microfilm Library, St. John's Abbey, Collegeville, Minnesota.

This book was originally published in Italian under the title *Bibbia e preghiera: La lectio divina* © 1990 by Editrice Àncora Milano. All rights reserved.

4   5   6   7   8   9

Library of Congress Cataloging-in-Publication Data

Magrassi, Mariano, 1930–
    [Bibbia e preghiera.   English]
    Praying the Bible : an introduction to lectio divina / by Mariano Magrassi ; translated by Edward Hagman.
        p.   cm.
    Includes bibliographical references.
    ISBN 0-8146-2446-4 (alk. paper)
    1. Bible—Reading.   2. Bible—Devotional use.   3. Spiritual life-
-Catholic Church.   I. Title.
BS617.M2713   1998
248.3—dc21   97-52992
                                                                CIP

Contents

To the Reader

This can be a disturbing book. After a first reading begun out of curiosity and with some misgivings, we end up reading it again out of a desire to absorb its contents more fully. Even before the council, we rightly reacted against a presentation of the Word of God that gave free rein to emotions, personal opinion, and pietism. Today's advances in biblical studies have become increasingly known even to non-specialists. In our reading of Scripture, they enable us to adhere to the literal sense, careful to situate the sacred texts in their original historical-religious context. We are proud of these achievements which now belong by right to all, whether believers or not.

But the very fact that we have these things makes our situation ambiguous. Either we become enclosed in our self-sufficiency or we open ourselves to communion. It is the constant back-and-forth between poverty and plenty. This book can be appreciated only by one who feels the limits of our present knowledge and the urgent need to incorporate it into a broader spiritual synthesis. It does not intend to present the ancients as a personal panacea but rather to introduce us to that faith climate in which for twelve centuries the Church read the Word of God. Archbishop Magrassi, with his vast knowledge of the Fathers and medieval monastic writers, has synthesized the various aspects that make up the unique and extraordinary experience of *lectio divina*.

What is it, what are its key ideas, what are the necessary personal dispositions, what are the steps by which prayed reading is transformed into genuine contemplation: these are the principal subjects discussed. If we really understand it, it is a discussion that contains a healthy challenge and an invitation to grow. To be sure, not everything in that way of reading the Bible was authentic. But the aberrations, linked to the tastes of a particular historical period, do not detract from the eternal validity of a faith experience that still captivates us today.

If we wish to be specific and explain the reasons for this fascination, there are two that must be stressed above all. First is what might be called the splendor of faith—faith that manifests its desire to see in a crescendo of suffering and love. Faith becomes contemplation of the mystery of Christ and the Church, which it has learned to discern and admire in the books of the Old and New Testament. It creates the "biblical" person from the spiritual and mental fibers impregnated with words, images, and reminiscences of the sacred text. Thus, contemplation is not a subjective experience of God but the fruit of a constant "yes" to revelation, an objective reality offered to us. It is something *other* than ourselves, even though it is *for* us. Contrary to what we might think at first, this is how the Fathers and medievals were able to avoid the dangers of too much introspection, sterile pietism, or a purely moralistic use of the Word. Second, *lectio divina*, a personal continuation of liturgical hearing of the Word, is not presented as a "spiritual exercise." It is a personal encounter with Christ, the one Word expressed in various ways, and it involves the whole person. Invited to a new exodus, the believer, as a member of the People of God, plays a leading role in the unique history of salvation. Here the Word is truly living and active, sharper than the most piercing sword. What rich affective expressions accompany this personal relationship with Christ! Often our dry meditations can only remain dumbfounded.

In conclusion, for the Fathers and monks there is no Christian life or Christian prayer that is not nourished daily—and in a certain sense exclusively—on Sacred Scripture. It is an idea that has been revived by the council and post-council, and for us it should be the *unum necessarium* (see DV 25; PC 6; *Ecclesiae Sanctae* 2, 16; *Venite seorsum* II). Perhaps we lack this because we are tempted to rationalize the Word of God, to make it so humanly obvious that it can be used to justify our philosophical and political choices. The Fathers, recognizing the Spirit as the author Scripture, ask its readers to be men and women of the Spirit and friends of Christ, even before they are perfect exegetes. And if we can recapture something of the Fathers' faith, surely their influence will have invigorated and protected us.

Abbreviations

ABSALON
    Serm.   *Sermon(s)*
Acta SS. O.S.B.   *Acta Sanctorum Ordinis Sancti Benedicti*
Acta Apost. Sedis   *Acta Apostolicae Sedis*

ADALGER
    Admon. ad Nonsuindam   *Admonition to a Recluse*
    reclus.

ADAM SCOTUS
    De trip. tab.   *On the Tripartite Tabernacle*

AELRED OF RIEVAULX
    De Jesu duod.   *On Jesus at Twelve Years Old*
    De oner.   *On the Burdens of Isaiah*
    Spec. charit.   *The Mirror of Charity*

ALAN OF LILLE
    Elucid. super Cant.   *Commentary on the Canticle of Canticles*

ALCUIN
    Epist.   *Letter(s)*
    In Ps.   *Commentary on the Psalms*

AMBROSE
    De off. ministr.   *On the Duties of the Clergy*
    In Luc.   *Commentary on the Gospel of Luke*
    In Ps.   *Commentaries on the Psalms*
    In Ps. CXVIII   *Commentary on Psalm 118*
    Serm.   *Sermon(s)*

AMBROSE AUTPERT
    In Apoc.   *Commentary on the Apocalypse*
Anecdota Mareds.   *Anecdota Maredsous*

ANSELM
   De concord.   *On the Harmony of the Foreknowledge,*
                                          Predestination, and Grace of God
                                          with Free Will

AUGUSTINE
   Confess.   *Confessions*
   De spir. et litt.   *On the Spirit and the Letter*
   Doctr. Christ.   *On Christian Doctrine*
   In Joann.   *Tractates on the Gospel of John*
   In Ps.   *Explanations of the Psalms*
   Serm.   *Sermon(s)*

BEDE
   In Marc.   *Commentary on the Gospel of Mark*

BERNARD
   De cons.   *Five Books on Consideration*
   De conv. ad clericos   *On the Conversion of Clerics*
   De div.   *Sermons on Various Occasions*
   Epist.   *Letter(s)*
   In Cant.   *Sermons on the Canticle of Canticles*
   In Epiph.   *Sermon on the Epiphany of the Lord*
   In Ezech.   *Commentary on Ezekiel*
   In Ps. Qui habitat   *On the Psalm "Qui habitat"*
   Liber de gr. et lib. arb.   *On Grace and Free Will*
   Serm. in adv.   *Sermon on the Coming of the Lord*

BONVAVENTURE
   Coll. in Hex.   *Conferences on the Six Days of Creation*

BONIFACE
   Epist.   *Letter(s)*

CAESARIUS OF ARLES
   In Apoc.   *Commentary on the Apocalypse*
cap.   chapter

CASSIAN
   Coll.   *Collationes [Conferences]*

CASSIODORUS
   In psalt.   *On the Psalter*

CCL   Corpus Christianorum. Series Latina

CLEMENT OF ALEXANDRIA
   Prot.   *Protrepticus [Exhortation to the Greeks]*
Cont. Med.   Corpus Christianorum. *Continuatio
                                      Medievalis*

DV   Vatican II, *Dei Verbum* [Dogmatic
                                      Constitution on Divine Revelation]

Ench. Bibl.   *Enchiridion Biblicum*

GARNERIUS OF ROCHEFORT
   Serm.   *Sermon(s)*
   Serm. de nativ. Dom.   *Sermon on the Nativity of the Lord*

GERHOH
   In Ps.   *Commentary on the Psalms*

GILBERT OF HOYLAND
   In Cant.   *Sermons on the Canticle of Canticles*

GODFREY OF ADMONT
   Hom. dom.   *Sunday Homilies*
   Hom. In Script.   *Homilies on Scripture*

GREGORY THE GREAT
   Epist.   *Letter(s)*
   In Cant.   *Homilies on the Canticle of Canticles*
   In Evang.   *Homilies on the Gospels*
   In Ezech.   *Homilies on Ezekiel*
   In Reg.   *Commentary on the First Book of Kings*
   Moral.   *Moral Discourses on Job*
   Mor., ep. miss.   *Moral Discourses on Job,
                                         Dedicatory Letter*
   Reg. past.   *Pastoral Rule*

HELINANDUS
   Serm.   *Sermon(s)*

HENRY OF MARCY
   De per. civ. Dei   *Tract on the Pilgrim City of God*

HERVE OF BOURG-DIEU
  In Cor.   Commentary on the First Letter to the
                             Corinthians

HILARY
  Tr. myst.   On the Mysteries

hom.   homily (-ies)

HONORIUS
  In Cant.   Commentary on the Canticle of Canticles
  In Ps.   Commentary on the Psalms
  Sp. Eccl.   The Mirror of the Church

HUGH OF METELLUS
  Epist. ad S. Bern.   Letter to St. Bernard

HUGH OF ST. VICTOR
  De arca Noe mor.   The Ark of Noah

IGNATIUS OF ANTIOCH
  Ad Philad.   Letter to the Philadelphians

INNOCENT III
  Serm. in fest. Jo. Bapt. Sermon on the Feast of St. John the
                             Baptist

IRENAEUS
  Advers. haer.   Against Heresies

IRIMBERT
  In Ruth prol.   Commentary on the Book of Ruth,
                             Prologue

ISIDORE
  Sent.   Three Books of Sentences

JEROME
  Epist.   Letter(s)
  In Eccles.   Commentary on Ecclesiastes
  In Gal.   Commentaries on the Letter to the
                             Galatians
  In Is.   Commentaries on Isaiah
  In Matt.   Commentaries on the Gospel of Matthew
  In Tit.   Commentaries on the Letter to Titus

JOHN CHRYSOSTOM
    In Gen.   Homilies on Genesis
    In Matt.   Homilies on the Gospel of Matthew

JOHN SCOTUS ERIUGENA
    De div. nat.   On the Division of Nature
    Hom. in prol. Joann.   Homily on the Prologue to the Gospel of
                                    John
    In Joann.   Commentary on the Gospel of John
    Super hier. coel.   Exposition of the Celestial Hierarchy

LECLERCQ, J.
    Anal. monast.   Analecta monastica

LEO THE GREAT
    Sermo   Sermon(s)

LG   Vatican II, Lumen Gentium [Dogmatic
                                    Constitution on the Church]

lib.   book

Max. Bibl. Vet. Patrum   Maxima Bibliotheca Veterum Patrum

MGH Auct. ant.   Monumenta Germaniae historica,
                                    Auctores antiquissimi

NICOLAUS OF CLAIRVAUX
    In Nativ.   Sermons on the Nativity of the Lord

OGER OF LOCEDIO
    Serm. de verbis Dom. in   Sermons on the Word of the Lord at the
        coena   Supper

ORIGEN
    In Cant.   Homilies on the Canticle of Canticles
    In Ex.   Homilies on Exodus
    In Gen.   Homilies on Genesis
    In Jer.   Homilies on Jeremiah
    In Joann.   Commentaries on the Gospel of John

In Jos.	*Homilies on Joshua*
In Luc.	*Homilies on the Gospel of Luke*
In Rom.	*Commentaries on Romans*

OTHLOH OF ST. EMMERAN
De cursu spir.	*On the Spiritual Course*

PASCHASIUS RADBERTUS
De fide	*On Faith, Hope, and Charity*
In Lam.	*Exposition of the Lamentations of Jeremiah*

PAULINUS OF NOLA
Epist.	*Letter(s)*
PC	Vatican II, *Perfectae caritatis* [Decree on the Appropriate Renewal of Religious Life]

PETER OF CELLE
Serm.	*Sermon(s)*

PETER THE VENERABLE
De mirac.	*On Miracles*

PETER LOMBARD
Serm.	*Sermon(s)*
PG	Patrologia Graeca

PHILIP OF HARVING
De dignit.	*On the Dignity of Clerics*
PL	Patrologia Latina
praef.	preface
proem.	preface

PSEUDO-AMBROSE
Serm.	*Sermon(s)*

PSEUDO-HUGH
In reg. S. Aug.	*On the Rule of St. Augustine*

RABANUS MAURUS
In Ezech.	*Commentary on Ezekiel*

RB	Rule of Benedict
Rech. de sc. relig.	*Recherches de science religieuse*
RICHARD OF ST. VICTOR	
In Apoc.	*Commentary on the Apocalypse*
RUPERT OF DEUTZ	
De glorif. Trin.	*On the Glorification of the Trinity and the Procession of the Holy Spirit*
De Trin.	*On the Trinity and Its Works*
De op. S. Spir.	*On the Works of the Holy Spirit*
In Ex.	*On Exodus*
In Gen.	*On Genesis*
De vict. Verbi Dei	*On the Victory of the Word of God*
In Apoc.	*Commentary on the Apocalypse*
In Eccles.	*Commentary on Ecclesiastes*
In Joann.	*Commentary on the Gospel of John*
In Mich.	*Commentary on Micah*
In Num.	*Commentary on Numbers*
In Oseam	*Commentary on Hosea*
In Zach.	*Commentary on Zechariah*
SC	Vatican II, *Sacrosanctum Concilium* (Constitution on the Sacred Liturgy)
SMARAGDUS	
Comm. in Reg. S. Ben.	*Commentary on the Rule of St. Benedict*
Diad. monac.	*Diadema monachorum*
Sourc. chrét.	Sources chrétiennes
THOMAS AQUINAS	
Sent.	*Commentary on the Sentences*
tit.	title
WILLIAM OF ST. THIERRY	
In Cant.	*Commentaries on the Canticle of Canticles*

╬ 1 ╬

Liturgical Proclamation and *Lectio Sacra*

"All . . . should immerse themselves in the scriptures by constant spiritual reading and diligent study . . . in order to learn 'the surpassing knowledge of Jesus Christ' (Phil 3:8) by frequent reading of the divine scriptures. 'Ignorance of the scriptures is ignorance of Christ'" (DV 25). These exhortations addressed by the council to all members of the people of God—clergy, religious and laity—deserve the utmost attention. Their reception determines to a great extent the success of the work of renewal begun by the council.

Many have insisted that without a corresponding biblical catechesis liturgical reform will end up a failure on the pastoral level. We will have renewed rites, but there will be no active, conscious, or full participation in them. That is not all. Biblical catechesis will not be able to plant the word of God in the hearts of the faithful unless it is so animated by diligent contact with that Word that its message becomes genuine "good news." Ministers of the word must not become "empty preachers of the word of God to others, not being hearers of the word in their own hearts."[1] Their goal must be to lead all the faithful, as the council says, to personal contact with the word which allows it to "speed on and triumph" in us. An old monastic rule used the striking expression, "To drink salvation

---

[1] Augustine, *Sermo* 179, 1 (PL 38, 966), cited in DV 25.

1

from Sacred Scripture in order to arouse a spirit of fervor."[2] In every biblical (and liturgical) proclamation, *lectio sacra* becomes the source from which the monk draws his fervor and the final end where he reaches full spiritual maturity.

Our subject is part of a bigger question that for some time has been the object of lively interest and heated debate. What is the relation between liturgy and the spiritual life, or as Jacques Maritain would say, liturgy and contemplation?[3] Reflection on this key question began in an atmosphere of arguments and misunderstandings. But it rediscovered the balance between liturgical and private prayer as well as their profound unity. Rediscovery of the patristic and medieval tradition played a major role in this. Following the same line, we would like to stress the vital continuity between these two moments in the Christian life: hearing the Word in ecclesial celebrations and private reading of the sacred text.

---

[2] *Regula Ferioli* or *Ferreoli Uzeticensis*, ch. 24 (Ed. Hostein-Brockie, *Codex Regularum* I, Graz 1957, 156f).

[3] The discussion became particularly heated with the work by Jacques and Raissa Maritain, *Liturgy and Contemplation*. It is a cry of alarm in defense of the contemplative ideal, threatened as they see it by the liturgical movement, toward which the two adopt a polemic stance. The effect of the book was to stir up a hornets' nest.

Vagaggini's classic work, *The Theological Meaning of the Liturgy*, had already appeared in 1957. It provided a clear and profound analysis of the question of the relationship between liturgy and mysticism. As a result, liturgists were particularly aware of the question. Many reviews reacted in timely fashion: *La vie spirituelle, Questions liturgiques et paroissiales, Worship, Revue Grégorienne*, and *Rivista di ascetica et mistica* which carried an article by Vagaggini in 1962. Maritain's argument rests on a basic misunderstanding. Participation in worship is reduced to something purely extrinsic, whereas contemplation, by contrast, is said to be achieved outside and independent of the celebration. In fact the act of worship is "contemplative," and although communal in nature, it calls for no less in terms of the believer's inner personal energy. Indeed, cultic contemplation must be said to be superior to private contemplation. This is a corollary of the thesis which states that liturgical prayer is superior to private prayer. All this can be concretely applied to that part of the question we are dealing with here.

Primacy of ecclesial hearing

Liturgical proclamation is obviously the place and privileged means of contact with the sacred text. There the living and active Word is returned to me in all its fullness. It is easy to show this based on a simple theological reflection.[4] The Word is living when the speaker is present and it is actually coming from his mouth. Only the presence of Christ prevents the Word from becoming a purely historical document. The Church can claim this presence because it is identified with Christ. It is his continuation, or as Bossuet would say, "It is Christ diffused and made known." But the mystery of the Church is actualized to the fullest in the celebration.

The liturgical assembly is not only a manifestation or epiphany of the great "people united in the unity of the Father, Son, and Holy Spirit," to quote Cyprian's famous definition borrowed by the council. It is also the very *culmen* of its actualization. Each local assembly is, as it were, a concentration of the great universal Church (see LG 26). And since the Church is the body of Christ, the full actualization of his mystery brings with it the fullness of the presence of the Risen One.

Seen thus, the words of the Constitution on the Sacred Liturgy stand out in bold relief: "It is he himself who speaks when the holy scriptures are read in church" (SC 7). There the Word is linked to the rite which is an action of Christ; there it rediscovers its original power as saving proclamation. The rites and texts of all liturgical traditions, both Eastern and Western (see, for example, the reverence paid to the Gospel book), stress this presence of the Lord. As the *Didache* admonishes: "Day and night remember him who preaches God's word to you, and honor him as the Lord, for where his lordship is spoken of, there is the Lord" (IV, 1). Or consider the introduction to the reading of the Gospel in the Armenian Rite where the deacon invites the people, "Let us be attentive," to which they respond, "God speaks." When it is God present who speaks, his

---

[4] Here we are summarizing principles enunciated in greater detail in *La Parola di Dio nell'assemblea liturgica,* Brescia 1966, 69–100.

Word retains its original power to save. It is a creative Word; it does what it says.

While drawing as many conclusions as we can from these principles, we must avoid undue exaggeration. To say with the council that the liturgy in all its parts is "the summit toward which the activity of the church is directed" (SC 10) does not mean that everything is reduced to liturgy. The council is equally clear in saying that "the sacred liturgy is not the church's only activity" (ibid. 9). The Church does not actualize its mystery or carry out its activity only in liturgical acts. It follows from this that in the liturgy the Word is living and active *maximally* though not *exclusively*. All other forms of preaching (missionary or catechetical, for example) involve the Church in some way and thus imply Christ's presence in the proclaimed Word. The one who transmits it is an apostle, according to the Jewish maxim: "The apostle of a person is, as it were, that person's other self."

Something similar must be said about private Bible reading. Of course the book itself is not the Word of God, only the means by which it is transmitted to me. But the reader of the book is a member of the Church. That reading takes place in the context of the ecclesial mystery, where the same Spirit who inspired the prophets and sacred writers is present and active. Therefore the text can be read "in the light of the same Spirit by whom it was written." If the Church is the body that preserves and transmits the living and active Word, then whoever lives in it and receives the biblical message from the hands of the one who possesses it as a living whole, is addressed by a divine Word in which God himself is present. Theology needs to reflect more deeply on this point. Here it is enough to state the general principle.

But this *living* character of the Word within the Church, wherever it may be heard, does not destroy the undisputed priority of the hearing that takes place where the Savior's presence reaches its culmination. Just as all ecclesial proclamation of the Word is directed toward liturgical proclamation as its final end, so all personal reading of the sacred text finds its center in liturgical hearing—as preparation for it, or as its continuation.

Lectio divina as preparation for liturgical hearing

First, as preparation. We know from daily experience that it is not enough to hear a biblical reading in order to automatically derive spiritual fruit from it. It is not the material sound of the syllables that is life-giving. The hearer must understand with an enlightened faith the meaning of the message God is conveying. The soul's doors must be opened to the One who makes himself lovingly available in his Word. Can this be done by one who has never picked up a Bible? The council would say that we must always have it in our hands. The discussion is similar to that usually had concerning the eucharistic bread. Received without preparation, without faith and love, the Bread of Life is no longer lifegiving. God's saving initiative is frustrated. God stops in front of doors that are shut.

There is another even more obvious reason. Although the reform may have given us "a richer table of the Word," of necessity the liturgy will always give us no more than biblical fragments—a *sacred page* as the ancients would say—which must be fit into the overall context of the passage and book in question. Even though the new Lectionary provides a broader selection, it does not give us the whole Bible. Besides, it touches only a few. For most Christians there are only the Sunday readings. The situation was different for the medieval monks who were less hurried than we. It is said that one day Abbot John of Gorze (10th cent.) had the whole book of Daniel read as the third lesson! The refectory readings continued those of the Office. In some Lectionary manuscripts, the text is marked to show where it was interrupted to be resumed at table.[5] Besides all this, the monastic legislators set aside several hours in the daily horarium for *lectio divina*, in which we know the Bible played a major part.[6] Thus it comes as no surprise to find that, given their familiarity with Scripture, these men were practically living concordances.

But monks or not, we, unfortunately, are far from this!

---

[5] See J. Leclercq, *La liturgia e i paradossi cristiani*, Milan 1967, 286.

[6] See A.M. Mundó, *Las Reglas monásticas latinas del siglo VI y la "lectio divina*," in *Studia monastica*, 9 (1967) 229–56.

The Breviary (as the name itself tells us) reduced the former readings to a summary. Personal contact with the sacred text had become the business of a few biblical scholars or contemplatives. We have seen the results in an impoverished theology and pastoral practice, which is increasingly removed from the authentic tenor of the Word of God. The council calls for reconversion.

The reform insures a better choice and greater variety in the liturgical readings. But obviously the Breviary will remain "abbreviated," and the Mass readings will need to consider the limits imposed by the pastoral situation. Other ages were tempted to make liturgical celebrations more wordy; today the trend is in the opposite direction—which is not to say this is necessarily bad. "Not to pray less but better" was the constant refrain of those who supported this trend at a meeting of abbots. But a summary retains its full meaning only because of what it summarizes. The "short reading" regains its full meaning when situated within a longer, private reading. Now that the temporal cycle gives us snippets, we must take it upon ourselves to read, in the same order, the books of the Bible from which these are taken. Only then will we be able to return to the biblical fullness of the past, even if we cannot (and should not) copy the liturgy of that time.

A need to go deeper and personalize the text

But it is not only a question of breadth; it is first a question of depth. The biblical text, even when accompanied by the homily, obviously does not reveal all its riches at first hearing. Much less can it sink immediately into the deeper part of human life and become a vital part of each one's inner world. Vital hearing requires loving, calm, reflective, personal poring over the text.

Once again a comparison with the eucharistic bread is instructive. We know how strongly ascetical practice, guided by church documents, including the latest,[7] insists on the need for

[7] See, for example, the instruction *Eucharisticum mysterium*, n. 38.

personal thanksgiving. It allows us to open ourselves to Christ's spiritual presence and action so that he might penetrate all our faculties and fill our life. The divine energy received in the sacrament becomes rooted in our soul. The demands of the Word are the same, since it forms a single table with the Eucharist. It is not enough to eat; we must assimilate, or as the ancients would say, "ruminate." Thus *lectio sacra* is the natural complement of ecclesial proclamation. There the soul digs deeper and deeper into the riches of an inexhaustible text. There it is surprised by those inner and often unexpected flashes that shed new light on the message. At last we perceive the true meaning of a text we have heard a thousand times before—a meaning that can nourish and direct an entire life. People experience this every day. We automatically think of the prologue to the Letter to the Ephesians. There Dom Marmion discovered what would be the central theme of his spiritual life, our adoption in Christ; there Sister Elizabeth of the Trinity discovered her call to be *laudem gloriae*.[8]

This leads us to another aspect of the question: going deeper becomes personalization. In the liturgy "God speaks to his people . . . and the people respond to God both in song and in prayer" (SC 33). The Word of the living God unites the entire community, which seals its union around the altar in the common hearing. Today we rightly insist on the communal nature of every liturgical act, indeed of the Christian life itself. This is in reaction to the highly individualistic formation of past centuries. But we must also remember the personal and unique nature of every encounter with God. Christian balance comes from a harmonious blend of the two elements. The Word of God is not exempt from this law. God speaks not only to his people; he also addresses me personally. His Word takes on a special tone and resonance for me, a function of the special and unique plan he has for my life. Thus the liturgy's universal dialogue becomes personal and unique in the *lectio sacra*

[8] See the two valuable studies by M.M. Philipon on these two leading figures in nineteenth-century spirituality: *La dottrina spirituale di Dom Marmion*, Brescia 1956; *La dottrina spirituale di Suor Elisabetta della Trinità*, Brescia 1957.

that is its continuation. What the Lord first said to all, I hear addressed to me. I hear a Word that responds to *my* problems, enlightens *my* steps, expresses *my* ideal.

Every truly contemplative life is shining proof of this essential process. We recall how Charles de Foucauld relived the mysteries of Christ following the text of the Gospel. That tête-à-tête with the divine Friend in which the soul overflows with warm and passionate words is as personal as one could imagine. But at the same time, every sincere God-seeking person experiences such contemplative urges. They are a continuation of the Church's celebration of the liturgical year in the sanctuary of the soul.

But Christian tradition offers examples where the vital link between liturgical hearing and personal meditation on the Word is even stronger. The figure most studied in this regard is St. Gertrude,[9] but the Middle Ages are full of others like her. These special cases reflect what was achieved by all in a more ordinary manner. They are people whose spiritual life resonates in perfect harmony with the objective realities presented to all the people of God in the liturgy.

Meditation, personal prayer, and mysticism spring from the Word found on the lips of the Church at prayer. They are constantly nourished at that source. St. Gertrude's "revelations" are typical in this regard. They are moments when what had previously been matter of faith became for her the object of certain experience. The Lord speaks to her. And what does she hear him say? The same words he spoke in the liturgy. When Gertrude tries to write down these experiences, her language is that of the Scripture texts from the day's liturgy. Here is a clear sign of personal meditation influenced by the liturgical word and inseparable from it.

In technical terms, the medievals would say that in the liturgy the Word reveals mainly its *allegorical* dimension (which refers to the mystery of Christ and the Church) and its *anagogical* dimension (which refers to the final consummation). In personal reading it reveals its *anthropological* dimen-

---

[9] See, for example, J. Leclercq, op.cit., 221–27; and C. Vagaggini, *Il senso teologico della Liturgia*, 4th ed., Rome 1965, 699–792.

sion (which refers to the individual's spiritual life). These senses, we know, are both *many* and *one*. They combine the various aspects of a single reality: the mystery of Christ lived at various levels. They are linked by an organic continuity. The Church and the individual are not two different realities—not just because the individual is part of the Church but because the entire mystery of the Church is in some way contained in every soul. Thus it is not an accomodation to hear the Lord's words to his Bride addressed to oneself.

The ancients were vividly aware of this. No separation or conflict can exist between the soul's dialogue with God and the Church's. We know that, in our own way, each of us is the whole Church; its mystery is relived in us. "Each of us is also the Church," says St. Bernard.[10] And in another place, "The Church, that is, the soul that loves God."[11] For Origen this identity becomes a dominant theme of exegesis. "I am the Church, I am the spouse," he repeats over and over. He sees in every believer's soul a "microcosm of the perfect Church." The City of God, Jerusalem, is both the Church whose architect is Christ and that inner, invisible dwelling built by him in the heart of each person.[12] Traditional commentaries on the Canticle (which was regarded as the heart of all Revelation) apply this principle more systematically. There we find expressed the shared consciousness of Tradition.[13]

This traditional conviction has proven surprisingly fruitful. We urgently need to make it our own today. If the soul is conscious of its identity with the mystery of the Church, it will spontaneously rediscover the close link between liturgical hearing and personal meditation. A kind of spiritual exchange

[10] Bernard, *Super Cant.*, 57, 3 (ed. J. Leclercq, II, 121).

[11] Idem, *Super Cant.*, 29, 7 (ed.cit., I, 248).

[12] Origen, *In Ex.*, hom. 9, n. 3-4 (PG 4, 237–44).

[13] See H. de Lubac, *Exégèse médiévale. Les quatre sens de l'Écriture*, part I, vol. II, Paris 1959, 560–61. The author rightly criticizes the claim of E. de Bruyne (*Études d'esthétique médiévale*, III, 31–32) that there are two quite distinct strands in the tradition: a "Christian Socratism" that comments on Scripture as a function of the spiritual life, and an "ecclesiastical" doctrine that situates it in a dogmatic and ecclesial context.

will take place. The soul, in its moments of prayer, will easily remain influenced by what moved it during the liturgy; it will relive it, probe it more deeply, personalize it in one-to-one dialogue with the divine speaker. On the other hand, what the soul experiences in these moments of prayer will, as it were, flow back to it as it listens during the liturgy. It will be totally present to the reading; it will listen more receptively and be more fully open. The two moments become complementary aspects of a single act.

The experience of Gregory the Great and the riches of the ancient tradition

The experience of St. Gregory the Great is particularly instructive. As pastor of the Church of Rome, he broke the bread of the Word for his people each day in the celebration; as a monk he made *lectio divina* one of the central exercises in his day, and as a saint he knew how to blend the two in perfect unity.

We might say that there are two phases to his experience. The first concerns the community. He feels that when he is explaining the Word to the community by his preaching, he is sustained and enlightened by the faith of his brothers and sisters. What was still unclear after solitary reflection is revealed to him within the community:

> For I know that in the presence of my brothers and sisters I have very often understood many things in the sacred text that I could not understand alone. . . . Thus it happens, by the grace of God, that as perception grows pride diminishes, since on your behalf I learn what I am teaching in your midst, for—I must confess—I often hear with you what I am saying.[14]

The community assumes the role of making the Word come alive. Understanding is a community act because dialogue itself is a community act. God does not speak to the hearts of individuals; he addresses himself to all.[15]

---

[14] Gregory, *In Ezech.* II, 1 (PL 76, 949).
[15] Idem, *Moral.* XXIII, 19, 34 (PL 76, 271).

The second phase is personal. Gregory seems to be speaking about an opposite experience. Now it is his private and solitary reading that introduces him to the secrets of the text and enables him to savor the Word of God:

> Often, through the grace of the almighty Lord, certain passages in the sacred text are better understood when the divine Word is read privately. The soul, conscious of its faults and recognizing the truth of what it has heard, is struck by the dart of grief and pierced by the sword of compunction, so that it wishes to do nothing but weep and wash away its stains with floods of tears. Meanwhile it is sometimes rapt in the contemplation of higher things and, in its desire for them, tormented by sweet weeping. . . . And because it still lacks the strength to cling to heavenly things, exhausted, it finds no rest save in tears.[16]

Despite the elegant style, we sense that this is not literature. Instead, Gregory is baring part of himself, sharing an intense experience. Note some of the soul's chief reactions as it listens: compunction for faults, contemplative rapture, intense desire for heaven. But in a liturgical setting, the first reaction is normally a resounding chorus of praise and thanksgiving. These other feelings are not excluded, however, and the dividing line is not all that clear. In any case, they are two complementary phases that influence each another. From their harmonious blend comes a total biblical experience.

Perhaps we moderns have lost the secret. Contact with the Protestant biblical piety of recent centuries may help us rediscover it. We are lucky to live in a serene ecumenical climate. We are able to see beyond obvious differences in the tradition of our separated brethren to undisputed values of traditional piety. One who lived these values before his conversion to Catholicism has left us this description:

> There exists a type of print or engraving, popularized by Dürer and later by Rembrandt, which expresses the essential element of this piety. We see a man or woman with the Bible open on their lap, hands folded, thoughts visibly absorbed in what they have read and in the God whom they have met in the reading.

---

[16] Idem, *In Ezech.,* loc.cit.

A personal and immediate encounter with him in the inspired Book has caused them to stop reading—as if overcome by the abundance of riches received—in order to gaze on him who speaks therein, to whom they respond as a child responds to its father or mother. . . . Direct familiarity with God, a heart-to-heart with him, created, maintained and constantly renewed by personal bible reading, followed by prayer to God, aware that this is above all a response to his Word: such is Protestant spirituality drawn from its source and seen in its vital center.[17]

It is the same attitude in which medieval monks are depicted in ancient miniatures. The practice of *lectio divina* in the cloister surely produced no less in terms of personal piety. But it had the advantage of a much livelier sense of the Church, later obscured in the Reformation. The example of the Reformation can inspire us to restore the Word to its rightful place in personal dialogue with God. But only the school of the ancient classics will teach us how to make this conversation part of the choral response of the people assembled, addressed and saved by God through his Word.

This is the tradition—created by the Fathers, continued and in some ways enriched by the experience of the medieval monks—whose basic insights we need to rediscover. We propose to do that here, but not as scholars intent on historically reconstructing the exegesis and *lectio* of the past.[18] Ours is a practical aim. We hope by contact with them to inject new life into the more-or-less scientific dryness of our reading. For the

[17] See L. Bouyer, *Parola, Chiesa e Sacramenti nel Protestantesimo e nel Cattolicesimo,* Italian tr., Brescia 1962, 11–12.

[18] In recent decades several well-reasoned studies, including monographs and syntheses, have been devoted to this topic. Among them must be mentioned the monumental work by H. de Lubac, already cited. Its four large volumes are an inexhaustible mine of texts, themes and traditional views. It is no longer possible to dismiss with a condescending smile this traditional contribution which shows such surprising richness and vitality. The Italian monks devoted a study congress to the topic "Bible and Spirituality" as seen throughout the tradition. But there are notable gaps. The *Proceedings* were published by the Daughters of St. Paul in the volume *Bibbia e spiritualità,* Rome 1967.

latter is no longer able to transform itself into prayer and become direct nourishment for our spiritual life. Let Augustine's
prayer rise from our hearts: "Let your scriptures be my chaste
delight."[19] We cannot, of course, always follow the ancients
through the maze of their allegorical interpretations. Nor can
we imitate their methods which, if we adopted them, would
ring false since they no longer come from the same spirit. It
would be like a Gothic church in the twentieth century. But we
will be able to adopt their faith vision and spiritual attitudes
in the presence of the Word. The soul's deepest needs before
God who gives himself in his Word do not change.

The chief values to be reclaimed seem to be these: a living
and coherent faith in the transcendence of God's Word; a sense
of Scripture's infinite fruitfulness and inexhaustible riches; a
deep admiration for the biblical world where beauty is a reflection of God's face and truth a foretaste of the vision toward
which he is leading us;[20] a profound sense of the unity of Scripture, so that everything is seen as a single, vast parabola,[21] one
great sacrament of the Christian realities;[22] above all, a way to
read it as a Word that is present and puts me in dialogue with
the God who is living and present; an ease in translating reading into prayer and using it to shed light on questions of existence in order to model my life on it; that presence of all my
soul's listening faculties which Claudel refers to when he
writes: "I take the Word to the letter. I believe one God who
swears by himself. God is Act, and all that he says forever is
forever actuality."[23]

And if we do not reach their level of fervor, we will at least
avoid turning our present aridity into theory. We will no
longer believe that a little historical criticism plus the deliber-
ate caution of our methods are enough to enter into the mystery of a Word that is divine Act.

[19] Augustine, *Confess.* XI, 2.3 [Tr. Maria Boulding].

[20] See Gerhoh, *In Ps.* XXI (PL 193, 990bc).

[21] See Rupert, *In Mich.* I (PL 178, 456a).

[22] See Leo the Great, *Serm.* 60, c. 1 (PL 54, 343–43); Hilary, *Tr. myst.* I, 1
(*Sourc. chrét.* 19, 74).

[23] *Paul Claudel interroge l'Apocalypse*, 332.

⊱ 2 ⊰

Lectio Divina: Meaning of the Term

The expressions *lectio divina* and *lectio sacra* are used extensively in fourth- and fifth-century patristic literature[1] in clear and concise sayings such as these:

> "The soul is fed each day with *lectio divina*" (Jerome);[2]

> "Intent on the food of *lectio divina*" (Ambrose, speaking about a Christian);[3]

> "*Lectio divina* raises us up . . ."; "That you may cultivate the fear of God through *lectio divina* and serious conversation" (Augustine)[4]

> "Therefore let us make time for *lectio divina*" (Hilary).[5]

The monastic rules give their blessing to this kind of *lectio*. It was one of the essential ascentic practices, and considerable time was set aside for it in the monk's daily plan.[6] As it became more widespread, references to its practice increase in the spiritual literature. It would take an entire poem to summarize

---

[1] See H. de Lubac, *Exégèse médiévale*, op.cit., vol. I, 82–84.
[2] Jerome, *In Tit.* III, 9.
[3] Ambrose, *In Luc.* IV, 20 (PL 15, 1618b).
[4] Augustine, *Serm.* 142, 1 (PL 38, 778); *Ep.* 20, 3 (PL 33, 87).
[5] Hilary, *Tractatus in CXVIII psalmum* (PL 9, 570a).
[6] See A.M. Mundé, *Las Reglas monásticas*, op.cit., 229–56.

15

Gregory the Great's teaching on the subject—a poem not de-
vised by the mind but created from living experience: "Each
day the breath of compunction filled my soul, consoled as I
was by diligent reading."[7] He has analyzed this experience,
leaving us wonderful descriptions.[8] Generations of medieval
monks learned from him and from the great Fathers (especially Origen, Jerome, and Augustine) how to make this exercise a source of light for the soul: "As light gladdens the eye,
so reading the heart."[9] But most of all they made it a source of
prayer: "It is Jacob's well from the water is drawn that irri-
gates prayer."[10]

There is one key idea in all this, repeated again and again: if
we speak to God in prayer, it is because God already speaks to
us first in the reading. "When we pray it is we who speak with
God, but when we read it is God who speaks with us."[11] This
was already a classic patristic principle. Jerome said: "If you
pray, you are speaking to your Spouse; if you read, he is speaking to you."[12] It is an exciting idea that caused one of many to
exclaim: "O sweet conversation, O delightful pastime."[13] The
council, in rediscovering the great traditional biblical values,
could not avoid repeating it. It did so with a quotation from St.
Ambrose.[14]

---

[7] Gregory, *Mor., ep. miss. (Sourc. chrét.,* 32, Paris 1952, 116).

[8] See, for example, *Mor.* 13, 20, 38 (PL 76, 274ab).

[9] Alcuin, *Epist.* 51 (PL 100, 216c).

[10] Idem, *Epist.* 1, (139a).

[11] Adalger, *Admon. ad Nonsuindam reclus.,* c. 13 (PL 134, 931c). From the
patristic era we have: Cyprian, *Ad Donatum,* 15: "Pray or read diligently;
now you should speak to God, now let God speak to you"; Jerome, *Epist.*
3, 4: "He listens to God when he reads Sacred Scripture; he speaks with
him when he prays to the Lord" (PL 22, 134). We have cited other medieval texts elsewhere: see M. Magrassi, *La preghiera a Cluny e a Citeaux,* in
La preghiera nella Bibbia e nella tradizione patristica e monastica, Rome 1964,
645–46.

[12] Jerome, *Epist.* 22, 25 (PL 22, 411).

[13] "*L'exhortation de Guillaume Firmat,*" ed. J. Leclercq, in *Anal. monast.* II
(*St. Anselm.,* 31) 397–404.

[14] Ambrose, *De off. ministr.* I, 20, 88 (PL 16, 50); see DV 25.

Before we attempt a more detailed analysis of traditional *lectio*, it would be well to spell out the meaning the term evokes. Some patristic texts give concrete examples, and their vivid descriptions enable us to re-experience the *lectio* of certain individuals. Thus Augustine describes for us how Ambrose used to come home, worn out from public life, and withdraw to a quiet place in his house. Spiritual hunger drew him to the pages of the sacred book: "When he read his eyes would travel across the pages and his mind would explore the sense, but his voice and tongue were silent." Augustine came in, but seeing him so completely engrossed he left, not daring to interrupt.[15] Paulinus of Nola describes Melania the Elder so absorbed in reading and so overcome with joy that she could no longer feel the hardness of the couch on which she was reclining.[16]

It is hard to find in our language a single term to convey the meaning of *lectio*. "Reading" is inadequate since that word refers to something too superficial and much too uninvolved. The term "study" is no better since it refers to something much more involved. Although it is an intellectual activity, it is too easily identified with scientific research or knowledge. In no way did the ancients intend to create for themselves through *lectio* a body of knowledge—not even theological or scriptural. The term "meditation" is closer, but as used in recent prayer methods it suggests something systematic or psychologically complicated. Such connotations were unknown to the ancients and equally unknown to the Church's school of prayer, the liturgy.

Is it possible to give a general idea with a formula that would somehow define it? Spiritual realities are rich and complex, to be sure, and not easily reducible to formulas. But some have attempted to sketch a definition. Guigo, the Carthusian, wrote that "reading is the careful study of the Scriptures, concentrating all one's powers on it."[17] This eloquent definition evokes the image of countless generations of monks in the quiet of their *scriptorium*, lovingly bent over the pages of the

---

[15] Augustine, *Conf.* 6, 3.

[16] Paulinus of Nola, *Epist.* 29, 13 (PL 61, 321).

[17] Guigo II, *Scala claustralium*, c. 1 (PL 184, 476b). [English tr. Dennis D. Martin].

Bible and the Fathers. But the definition is really quite generic and tells us nothing about its innermost nature. Genius for definitions was not a mark of the ancients; instead of analyzing these realities they lived them.

We find that Leclercq's definition, brief and concise as it is, gets to the heart of the matter: *"Lectio divina* is prayed reading."[18] Bouyer has attempted a more detailed description:

> It is personal reading of the Word of God during which we try to assimilate its substance; a reading in faith, in a spirit of prayer, believing in the real presence of God who speaks to us in the sacred text, while the monk himself strives to be present in a spirit of obedience and total surrender to the divine promises and demands.[19]

These words are meant to sum up the traditional attitude in the presence of the Word as found in the Fathers and in the whole monastic tradition.

Dom Paul Delatte, a great monk and abbot of Solesmes, was as familiar with this monastic tradition as the authors cited. Here is his analysis:

> *Lectio divina* is the organized totality of those progressive intellectual methods by which we make the things of God familiar to us and accustom ourselves to the contemplation of the invisible. Not abstract, cold speculation, nor mere human curiosity, nor shallow study; but solid, profound, and persevering investigation of Truth itself. We may say that God alone is the object of this study, its inspiration and its chief cause; for it is not only pursued under his gaze, but in his light and in very intimate contact with him. It is a study pursued in prayer and in love. The name *lectio* is only the first

---

[18] See J. Leclercq, *L'amour des lettres et le désir de Dieu (Initiation aux auteurs monastiques du moyen-âge)*, Paris 1957, 72; Idem, *Lecture et oraison*, in *La vie spirituelle*, May 1954, 392–401; Idem, *La lecture divine*, in *La Maison-Dieu*, n. 5 (1946) 22–23; Idem, J.P. Bonnes, *Un maître de la vie spirituelle au XIᵉᵐᵉ siècle, Jean de Fécamp*, Paris 1946, 97–103; Idem, *La spiritualité de Pierre de Celle* (1115–83), Paris 1946, 99–107, etc.

[19] L. Bouyer, *Parola, Chiesa e Sacramenti nel Protestantesimo e nel Cattolicesimo*, Italian tr., Brescia 1962, 17.

moment of an ascending series: *lectio, cogitatio, studium, meditatio, oratio, contemplatio.*[20]

Perhaps the ancients would have found the first part of this description too intellectual. But they would have easily seen themselves in the second part, which stresses the living presence of God who initiates the dialogue and plays the role of principal agent, and with whom the reader is associated in a kind of synergy. Dumontier also insists on this point in that impassioned tone of his, which is due to the fact that he is very familiar with the Cistercian school and perfectly in tune with it. He tries to explain the adjective *divina*, noting that it has not only an objective meaning: reading whose object is God's books or Word, but also a subjective meaning: reading done by two people, with God, a heart-to-heart with him. Even more, it is reading that bears a love message for me from the *God who seeks me* (one of Bernard's favorite expressions). On reaching the soul, it causes it to taste God, and it creates a personal bond with him. Then the soul experiences the truth of the psalm verse, a favorite in monastic literature: "Taste and see that the Lord is good."[21]

Others try to specify more the part of psychology and grace in reading. Certainly it is not enough to speak of *intellectual processes*. Love is also a coefficient of knowledge, especially in the life of faith. It often goes beyond the limits imposed by the intellect: "Love and knowledge" as the medievals would say,[22] anticipating Pascal's "reasons of the heart." The work of the affective faculty must be placed alongside that of the intellect, and above them the light of faith which transforms both and allows the soul to enter the divine world. Then everything converges in "a profound and peaceful gaze upon the invisible world"[23] through that Word which is "a lamp for our steps"on our journey to the living God.

[20] P. Delatte, *Commentaire sur la Règle de Saint Benoît*, Paris 1948, 348–49 [English tr. Justin McCann].

[21] P. Dumontier, *Saint Bernard et la Bible*, Paris 1953, 50, 86.

[22] This is the title of a study by J. Dechanet on William of St. Thierry and St. Bernard in *Revue du moyen-âge latin* 1 (1945) 349–54.

[23] See G. Colombas - L. Sansegundo - O. Cunill, *San Benito. Su vida y su Regla*, Madrid 1954, 463–64.

Given the seriousness and commitment demanded by such reading, we are no longer surprised to find that the ancients had great confidence in its spiritual effectiveness. Here, for example, is the witness of Smaragdus. It reflects the common understanding:

> For those who practice it, the experience of *lectio sacra* sharpens perception, enriches understanding, rouses from sloth, banishes idleness, orders life, corrects bad habits, produces salutary weeping and draws tears from contrite hearts . . . curbs idle speech and vanity, awakens longing for Christ and the heavenly homeland. It must always be accompanied by prayer and intimately joined with it, for we are cleansed by prayer and taught by reading. Therefore, whoever wishes to be with God at all times must pray often and read often, for when we pray it is we who speak with God, but when we read it is God who speaks with us. Every seeker of perfection advances in reading, prayer and meditation. Reading enables us to learn what we do not know, meditation enables us to retain what we have learned, and prayer enables us to live what we have retained. Reading Sacred Scripture confers on us two gifts: it makes the soul's understanding keener, and after snatching us from the world's vanities, it leads us to the love of God.[24]

Now that we have shed some light, in summary fashion, on the meaning of the term, we must analyze its components. That is to say, we must identify the main themes of traditional spirituality in the presence of the Word of God as encountered in *lectio divina*.

---

[24] Smaragdus, *Comm. in Reg. S. Benedicti,* ad cap. 4, n. 56 (PL 102, 784).

3

Lectio Divina: Key Ideas

Life is governed by ideas; practical applications are dictated by basic concepts. It is these we must identify first of all. We must find those great images of faith in which the ancients saw the message entrusted by God to the Scriptures. *How* they read depends on these more than anything else.

The majesty of Scripture

What was the Bible for the ancients? The answer, of course, cannot be summed up in one word, for the images are many and include the greatest of the human and divine worlds. The danger for us, with our critical minds, is that the text will become a history book, even though God is its protagonist and its subject is his marvels. For the ancients, "the text breathes" as Paul Claudel would say. Beneath its formulas they saw his mysterious presence. Scripture is God present who speaks to me.[1] When I hear his words, it is as if I could see his mouth.[2] More precisely, when I go beyond the letter of Scripture to its spirit, I personally encounter the living Christ. He is present to explain his own Word, which is gradually revealed to the eyes

---

[1] See H. de Lubac, *Exégèse médiévale*, op.cit., I, 83–84.
[2] Gregory, *Moral.* XVI, 25, 43 (PL 75, 1142).

21

of faith.[3] Understanding the Bible is like having a conversation with him.[4]

From this basic conviction comes a flood of images to express the Bible's meaning for the spiritual life. It is like a letter written to us by God to manifest his secrets,[5] a mirror that reveals to us our inner face,[6] a wheat field that nourishes the spirit,[7] a priceless treasure.[8] The Bible is a source of life for those who are dead in sin, a lamp to light the footsteps of those who walk in the darkness of this life,[9] a well allows us access to the depths of its hidden meaning and admits us to contemplation.[10] That is why it is a consolation to mystics, rest in God, and a source of living water.[11] At this table set for us by Christ, our whole spiritual life is nourished: "Sacred Scripture is the table of Christ . . . where we are fed, where we understand what we must love and what we must desire, and to whom we must lift up our eyes."[12]

" ' ource of living water," says John of Fecamp. But what exactly is this living water? A chorus of answers comes from all sides, vibrant as the experience from which they flow. "We drink from the fountain of divine knowledge," exclaims Rupert of Deutz, who spent his whole life in the pages of the Bible.[13] Richard of St. Victor stresses the brilliance of this divine knowledge.[14] Pseudo-Ambrose calls it an eternal word:

In Evang. II, 23, 1 (PL 76, 1182). *In Ezech.* I, 7 (PL 76, 844–48).

[4] Guuoh of St. Emmeran, *De cursu spirituali*, 21 (PL 146, 313).

[5] Gregory, *Epist.* V, 46; *Reg. Greg.* I, 345: "What is Sacred Scripture if not a letter from almighty God to his creatures?"

[6] Idem, *Moral.* II, 1 (PL 75, 553).

[7] Op.cit., VI, 5 (732).

[8] Op.cit., VI, 10 (735).

[9] Isidore, *Sent.*, III, 40 (PL 80, 896–97). Gregory, *Reg. past.* III, 24: "That they may consider that Sacred Scripture is a lamp for us in the night of the present life" (PL 76, 94a); Idem, *Moral.* XXVI, 16, 26 (PL 76, 362–63).

[10] Isidore, *Sent.*, III, 40 (PL 80, 897).

[11] See J. Leclercq - J.P. Bonnes, *Un maître de la vie spiritualle*, op.cit., 214–15.

[12] Alcuin, *In Ps.* 127 (PL 100, 630).

[13] Rupert of Deutz, *In Apoc.* XII (PL 169, 1203).

[14] Richard of St. Victor, *In Apoc.* VII, 5 (PL 196, 867cd).

". . . when we receive from the divine Scriptures the food of the eternal word. . . ."[15] It is "a foretaste of the food of truth that will be set before us at the table of heaven."

This is not speculative, abstract knowledge; it is saving knowledge. The experience of tradition confirms Paul's words to Timothy:

> All scripture is inspired by God and is useful for teaching, for reproof, for correction, and for training in righteousness, so that everyone who belongs to God may be proficient, equipped for every good work (2 Tim 3:16-17).

It is knowledge for life, capable of transforming our entire inner self and "restoring strength to our heart.[16]

Given these premises, we can see why the ancients might be unable to contain their enthusiasm for the sacred Book. They get excited when speaking about it and their words are moving. Rupert loves to talk about the "majesty of Scripture."[17] Human language pales before the transcendence of the Word; it loses all its zest and clarity unless sweetened by the salt of the "heavenly letter."[18] "The heavenly page reigns," sings one of the pre-scholastics in a poem.[19] These expressions are not the casual remarks of an exegete. They are quasi-technical and adopted by common use. People spoke of the *divina pagina, sacra pagina, pagina celeste, pagina eterna,* etc.[20] That page lies far higher than the poor fruits of human ingenuity, in a divine region that exceeds the bounds of heaven. It is a perfect act of faith. In today's world such an act of faith is harder. If systematic application of scientific categories to the Bible—from literary genres to *Formgeschichte*—can yield valuable results, it can

---

[15] Pseudo-Ambrose, *Serm.,* 27 (PL 17, 662a).

[16] Pseudo-Hugh, *In reg. S. Aug.,* c. 4 (PL 176, 894a).

[17] See *In Apoc.* III (PL 169, 908a). *De vict. Verbi Dei* X, 21 (PL 169, 1438c) etc.

[18] See Aelred, *De amicitia,* I (PL 195, 662a).

[19] See A. Neckam, *De naturis rerum libri duo, with the Poem of the same Author, De laudibus divinae sapientiae,* edited by Thomas Wright, London 1863, 453.

[20] H. de Lubac, op.cit., I, 84–85 amply documents these expressions.

also weaken that living sense of the Word's transcendence. Of what use would be all our scientific tools if they destroyed the basic values? That would not be a step forward but a step backward. In the presence of divine realities (such as the Word) what counts most is faith. It alone can lead us into the mystery. Everything else matters only if it is part of this atmosphere and functions within it.

Henri de Lubac, who is amazingly familiar with the ancients and who also has a good knowledge of modern exegesis, discreetly observes in a footnote:

> M.A. Gelin writes, with regard to the book of Ezekiel: "The passages about Tyre are the most well-known because of the information they give us about international trade."[21] It is a statement of fact. But that fact presupposes in our contemporaries a certain scale of values quite different from that of the people of the Middle Ages.[22]

A kiss of eternity

The ancients insisted especially on the link between Scripture and the beatific vision. The subject was so important that it led to a separate division in the classification of the scriptural senses: the anagogical.[23] Rabanus Maurus does not hesitate to say that Scripture "opens to us the gates of the heavenly kingdom."[24] To understand it here below is already a "kiss of eternity,"[25] adds William of St. Thierry.

This is a bold view and there are many nuances, depending on the various spiritual currents. But all are unanimous in stressing the relationship. Pope Gregory sums up the general

---

[21] This comment is from A. Robert - A. Feuillet, *Introduction à la Bible*, I, Paris 1957, 545.

[22] See H. de Lubac, op.cit., I, 487, n. 3.

[23] See the beautiful chapter on this subject in H. de Lubac, ibid. I, 621–43.

[24] Rabanus, *In Ezech.* XIV (PL 110, 894b).

[25] See William of St. Thierry, *In Cant.* n. 36 (*Sourc. chrét.*, 82, Paris 1962, 120).

thinking in these words: "When Scripture recounts eternal events as though they were happening in time, it causes those who are accustomed to temporal thoughts to pass imperceptibly to those of eternity."[26] When we study the sacred text, we feel as if we had already left the land of slavery to enter the land of freedom and knock at the doors of the kingdom.[27] Reading is seen as an anticipated vision of divine glory.[28]

But these statements are much too serious not to require further clarification. There are two ways of seeing the relation. The first considers the letter of Scripture and its many teachings. It distinguishes between the Word and the joyful object contemplated by the blessed. Thus Augustine distinguishes between the Gospel and its giver.[29] Viewed this way, the relation is based on a clear distinction. Our meditation on Scripture here below differs from face-to-face contemplation of the Word, which is reserved to the blessed who drink from the very source of Wisdom.[30] Then we will understand Scripture fully, but by that very fact it will be abolished. "Will the Gospel really be read aloud in that land where we shall contemplate the Word of God himself?" asks Augustine.[31] It remains true, of course, that our understanding of Scripture is ordained to that supreme contemplation where we shall see its author face to face.

We can also view the relation from the opposite side, as does John Scotus Eriugena.[32] Considering the very essence of Scripture, we can say that the Logos is one: it is both "Word" and "Speech." Then the distinction will be less clear, with only an ascending degree of difference between the two terms. Here on earth my search for God's face is part of my effort to interpret God's Word. In heaven my joy will consist in fully understanding that Word. That is why, as Rupert says, "to

---

[26] Gregory, *Moral.*, II, 20, 35 (PL 183, 148b).
[27] Bernard, *In Epiph.* II, 2 (PL 183, 148b).
[28] Idem, *In Ezech.* I, 8 (PL 76, 862).
[29] Augustine, *In Joann.*, tract. XXII, 2 (CCL 36, 223).
[30] Origen, *In Joann.* XIII, 5–7 (PG 13, 230–31).
[31] Augustine, *In Ps.* 83, n. 8 (CCL 39, 1153).
[32] John Scotus Eriugena, *De div. nat.* V, 38 (PL 122, 1010bc).

understand with our mind the mysteries of Scripture and to live them is already to reign in the kingdom of God."[33] The mystery of Scripture is the mystery of the kingdom of God. Among the others who say this is the great Jerome: "The kingdom of heaven is knowledge of the Scriptures."[34] Alcuin says that "to read the Scriptures is already to experience holy beatitude."[35]

Certainly the two views are not opposed. Combined, they clarify the concept, and at times we find them in the same author. The first view considers the written book; the second considers the living Gospel, that "divine Gospel we shall read forever in heaven,"[36] now concealed beneath the veil of words. As Bernard would say, it considers not merely a word that "sounds in the ear" but "a visible Word that our eyes may see him, a tangible Word that our hands may hold him," not "a written and silent word, but a Word incarnate and living."[37] This living Book, quite obviously, will not be abolished in heaven. It will present itself to our hungry eyes, which long to see him in the splendor of his beauty and truth. Only then will we understand this Word, for then we shall see him as he is.

Meditating now on Scripture, the eyes of faith seek to discover the same Word. And in that highest form of prayer, which tradition calls contemplation, they will even reach it. Later we must explain the relation between reading and contemplation. Ambrosius Autpertus says that the soul is "lifted up by an eternal spirit . . . to contemplate the divine myster-

---

[33] Rupert of Deutz, *In Apoc.* III (PL 169, 904b). *De Trinit., De op. Spir. Sancti* I, 6: "When we read Sacred Scripture, we are handling the Word of God; we have before our eyes the Son of God as in a mirror, indistinctly" (PL 167, 1575d).

[34] Jerome, *In Matt.,* (PL 29, 90). See Godfrey of Admont, *Hom. dom.* 23 (PL 174, 154d). Innocent III, *Serm.* 18 *in fest. Jo. Bapt.:* "The violent are taking the kingdom of heaven by force: they understand the mysteries of Scripture" (PL 217, 540c).

[35] Alcuin, *Liber de virtutibus et vitiis,* 5 (PL 101, 616).

[36] J. J. Olier, *Explications des cérémonies de la grand'messe de paroisse,* 1687, 407–8.

[37] Bernard, *Super missus est* IV, 11 (PL 183, 86b).

ies as though through the crevices."[38] The soul is lifted so high above itself "that it is carried off to the house of God."[39] It is fascinating, this journey by which the soul is led into the divine realm. But it begins with the reading of the sacred Books. All this, however, takes place in the darkness of faith. It is not yet vision, or perhaps we could say it is "incipient" vision. Perfect contemplation, full anagogy, is reserved for heaven: "Contemplation begun with most ardent love can never end."[40] Rupert, in his picturesque way, would say that we advance like explorers, Scriptures in hand, to the land of the living, but we do not fix our abode there.[41] To the eyes of faith, God's face shines dimly in the shadows, but it is not yet revealed in all its splendor. And so we must continue to seek it in the pages of Scripture: "When love grows, the search for what has already been found also grows."[42]

A living Book

We have been speaking of a Word or living Book. It is Jesus Christ, the object of all Scripture. But tradition regards the written text itself as living. This is one of the deeper faith insights that animates *lectio divina*. It derives from a concept of inspiration perhaps less technical than ours, but definitely richer. It can be documented in many of the great Fathers. For them, inspiration is not just something that acted once on the sacred writers, resulting in the inspired texts. It is an ongoing and ever-present influence at work within the Books themselves, which are and remain inspired. The presence of the Spirit who once dictated the Scriptures insures their perennial youth (to borrow a phrase from Irenaeus) and continues to

---

[38] Ambrosius Autpertus, *In Apoc.* I (*Max. Bibl. Vet. Patrum*, XIII, Lyons 1677, 429d).

[39] Peter Lombard, *Serm.*, in B. Haureau, *Notices et extraits* 32 (1888) 122.

[40] Ambrosius Autpertus, *In Apoc.* I (*Max. Bibl. Vet. Patrum*, XIII, Lyons 1677, 496ef).

[41] Rupert of Deutz, *De Trin., In Num.*, I, 37 (PL 167, 874–75).

[42] Augustine, *In Ps.* 104, n. 3 (CCL 40, 1537).

breathe life into them. They remain filled with the Spirit of God[43] and are constantly and "miraculously made fruitful by him."[44] This concept can rightly be compared to creation. It involves not only an initial act of God who draws creatures out of nothing; it also involves God's continuous presence by his power. Theology calls this "preservation," but in fact it is continuous creation. Things exist because at every moment God communicates existence to them, a little at a time. Augustine said: "For he did not create them and then go away: they are from him but also in him."[45] But is not the Word a creation of the Spirit? Could the Spirit possibly give it life and then abandon it?

Since it is a living word, Scripture implies the presence of the lifegiving Spirit and the Word of God expressed therein. The Spirit's instruments, from Moses to John, are of course dead; their task is finished. But the task of the Word of God and his Spirit is not finished. He is present on every page, still speaking to us and revealing his power from beginning to end, touching the depths of our soul like the edges of the universe. We will devote the next section to the presence of Christ in the Scriptures. Here we must explain the Spirit's presence. Our guide will be Gregory the Great, who has treated the subject with that persuasive style which is his hallmark.

For Gregory, inspiration (which he calls prophecy) is closely related to the spiritual life of the believer who pores over the inspired page. Prophet and believer are both touched by the Spirit: "Just as the Spirit of life touches the mind of the prophet, he also touches the mind of the reader." Of course Gregory does not mean to say these two "touches" are the same—only that the same Spirit is present in both.

Commenting on the vision of Ezekiel in which the symbolic chariot appears, he writes:

> The Spirit of life is in the wheels, because through the divine words we are given life by the gift of the Spirit. . . . God

[43] Origen, *De principiis* IV, 1, 7 (PG 11, 355–56).
[44] Anselm, *De concord.*, q. III, c. 6 (PL 157, 528b).
[45] Augustine, *Conf.*, IV, 12, 18.

touches the soul of the reader in various ways and degrees;
through the words of the sacred text he now arouses its zeal
. . ., now calms it and leads it to patience, now instructs it for
preaching, now pricks it to tears of repentance.[46]

It is a *living* Word because it is animated by the Spirit of life.
It is a lifegiving Word because, in the Spirit, I drink at the
very source of divine life. St. Bernard would later say: "I know
that by these things we live, and in all these [words] is the life
of my spirit."[47] Entering the human heart, his divine touch sets
its strings vibrating. He draws from them a variety of sounds,
from zeal to compunction, which blend into a marvelous spiritual symphony. Between the sacred author, moved by the
Spirit to write the text, and the reader, moved by the same
Spirit when reading it, a deep communion is established.
Time's differences do not matter because both are in communion with the Word of the living God. This view is not Gregory's alone. It began with Jerome when he wrote that the
Bible must be read and interpreted "in the light of the same
Spirit by whom it was written."[48] Medieval tradition accepts
this view and probes it endlessly. Here is how William of St.
Thierry expressed it in the twelfth century:

> The Scriptures must be read in the light of the same Spirit by
> whom they were written; they must also be understood in the
> light of the same Spirit.[49]

[46]Gregory, *In Ezech.* hom. VII, I, 9–16 (PL 76, 844–48).

[47]Bernard, *In Cant.* XVI, 1 (PL 183, 849a).

[48]Jerome, *In Gal.*, 5, 19–21 (PL 26, 417a). In the preface to his third edition
of the *Letter to the Romans* (1922), Barth evidently feels that the exegete is
faced with an either-or situation. Either, knowing what he is dealing with,
he places himself in a relation of loyalty to his author and writes his commentary, not *on* Paul but *with* Paul, for he feels responsible for what the
Apostle writes; or, like an irresponsible spectator, he decides to write his
commentary *on* Paul. Barth, for his part, maintains that no writer can be
made to speak again nor can his message be brought to life unless we
place ourself in a relation of loyalty to him. See K. Barth, *Römerbrief,* 4th
ed., 1924, XXff.

[49]William of St. Thierry, *Epistola ad fratres de Monte Dei*, I, X, 31 (PL 184,
327d).

Three stages of Scripture are envisioned here, each marked by the presence of the Spirit: its writing, which takes place in virtue of the Holy Spirit; our reading the sacred page, which must take place in virtue of the same Spirit; our deeper understanding, which creates within our soul the same sentiments as those of the Spirit of God. This is the unity of spirit mentioned by Paul (1 Cor 6:17). It is a profound view, echoed in recent magisterial documents[50] and in those of the council as well.[51]

In the words of Irenaeus, the continuing presence of the Spirit constantly "rejuvenates" the Word. It is the youth of continuous creation. Gregory has some marvelous things to say in this regard:

> Contemplation enables us not only to understand Scripture that is already written, but even to write if it does not yet exist, and then dispose ourselves daily to carry out God's will through its teachings.[52]

As described here by Gregory, contemplation is a Christian experience, rooted in love. It continues God's historical plan of salvation in each of us. When genuine, it is directly inspired by the Spirit and exists in radical dependence on the written Word of God. It sees itself in the Word and gives it new meaning. In this contemplative experience, Scripture is in a sense re-created. So true is this that if it did not already exist, it would be created now. What better way to express the original freshness of a Word that lives again in every vital Christian experience?

Vatican II follows the same line when it says that, through the Spirit, the living voice of the Gospel continues to ring out in the Church. It is not a Word from the past; God does not cease to speak.[53] To the degree that we read this living Word,

---

[50] Benedict XV, *Encyclical Spiritus Paraclitus*, 15 September 1920, *Ench. Bibl.* 469.

[51] DV 12.

[52] Gregory, *In Reg.*, III, 5, 30 (PL 79, 216c).

[53] DV 8.

the other ecclesial realities, such as theology, experience perpetual youth.[54]

This aspect of the theology of the Word was particularly well expressed by Karl Barth. His formulation contains the best of the Protestant experience, which on this point is in continuity with the best patristic tradition.

He distinguishes the Word of God from the human expressions in which it comes to us, even if these are chosen by the Spirit. The written word is only the means by which God's living Word reaches me, the divine act by which he addresses me, questions my whole existence and saves me. Paul would say it is "the power of God for salvation to everyone who has faith" (Rom 1:16). It not only transmits a message; it is a presence, a Person.

> Barth sees the Word as an act of God who seeks us and pursues us, a creative and recreative act offering us immediate contact with the world of the new creation in Christ. He sees the Word as God's presence among us, and finally, as the very Person of God made flesh.[55]

Thus he cannot understand the attitude of those who read the Bible as an interesting book, but one which does not concern them. No one can stand before the Word as a spectator.[56] I must grasp the full "dramatic" value of this Word as a Person who reveals himself to my openness, challenging me to commit myself to him. This is not simply an encounter with a piece of writing, even though divine. It is an encounter with the living God.

The saving power of God

Since it constantly receives life from the indwelling Spirit, the Word contains in itself the power to save. Paul describes it

---

[54] Ibid. 24.
[55] L. Bouyer, *Parola, Chiesa e Sacramenti*, op.cit., 18.
[56] See K. Barth, *Dogmatique*, French tr., vol. I, t. II, 75, 118.

as "the power of God for salvation to everyone who has faith" (Rom 1:16). It is not only truth; it is power. It not only teaches; it is at work in us. It not only shows us models to imitate; it causes us to act. Only recently has the theology of the Word[57] rediscovered this aspect of the Bible. But it is central in the traditional concept, as is clear from the many texts already cited. As one monastic rule puts it, "We drink salvation from Sacred Scripture."[58]

For this reason the Fathers have only to reverently ponder the same statements in the Bible. No other aspect is more strongly emphasized. The Bible presents the Word of God charged with creative power. Creatures respond to its call by taking their place in the cosmos: "Let there be light, and there was light." The power of the Word is irresistible because it is linked to the spirit-breath of God: "It is I who say to the deep: 'Be dry—I will dry up your rivers'" (Isa 44:27). It is a word that "does not return" (Isa 44:23; 55:10-11). The Gospels show us Christ commanding the winds and waves, fevers and demons, and his command is powerful, irresistible.

In the cosmos this power is more spectacular, but its action in human life is more profound. When it enters human life, the Word creates the course of history and stamps it with God's seal, making it a sacred history. Here the Word acts by entering the human heart, enabling it to respond freely to God's initiative. It becomes a collaborator with him in the advent of salvation. The divine word permeates the dough of human history like an active element with its complex reactions. It is not merely prediction. Standing at the crossroads of human decisions, its power animates and directs them toward their final end. And when the Word drops into someone's life and that person is seized with the prophetic charism, then he or she is inwardly transformed, his word is confirmed, his prediction is fulfilled (Isa 44:26). That person is introduced to the divine Word in all its power: "The Lord called me before I was

---

[57] See L. Alonso Schökel, *La Parola ispirata,* Italian tr., Brescia 1967, 320–56; O. Semmelroth, *Wirkendes Wort,* Freiburg 1962; H. Volk, *Zur Theologie des Wortes Gottes,* Münster 1962.

[58] *Regula Ferioli,* loc.cit., see chapter 1, note 2.

born, while I was in my mother's womb he named me. He made my mouth like a sharp sword" (Isa 49:2).

This power reaches its peak on the lips of Christ. His word has the power to restore life: "Lazarus, come out." He gives a man a new name and makes him an apostle. He restores in an instant the wasted flesh of a leper by an act of his will expressed in a word: "I will; be clean." He rebuilds a man's life and renews him within by his efficacious forgiving word: "Your sins are forgiven." He traveled the roads of Palestine "powerful in words and works." His words "will not pass away." The risen Christ lives on in his Church, and with him lives his word in the Gospel, now the word of the glorified Christ. And if, as Paul says, the resurrection established him in power and made him a "lifegiving spirit," his Word is also transformed. It is not weakened but strengthened. The gift of his Spirit intervenes. Under his influence, the Word can be better understood. It also penetrates more deeply, like a cutting sword, to that mysterious point where the supernatural spirit is joined to our vital principle: "Indeed, the word of God is living and active, sharper than any two-edged sword, piercing until it divides soul from spirit, joints from marrow" (Heb 4:12). Living, active, cutting, piercing: the rapid succession of adjectives gives the very rhythm of the sentence an impressive power, a faithful reflection of the saving word's activity. It is the imperishable seed from which the children of God are reborn (1 Pet 1:22-25). It is the power of God at work (Rom 1:16), "for those who believe" adds Paul. Indeed, it presupposes hearers who can open the doors of their soul through faith to receive the gift.

The spirituality of the ancients was deeply imbued with this revealed teaching. Their devotion to the Bible was based on this faith vision. There is found its energy and fire: "Indeed, these letters must be sacred, for they make us not only holy but also divine," exclaims Clement of Alexandria.[59] Chrysostom echoes him: "Even if the phrase is short, its power is great. Often, one word taken from there is enough to

---

[59] Clement of Alexandria, *Prot.*, 9, (PG 8, 197).

serve as viaticum for an entire lifetime."[60] Ephrem, with the imagination of a poet, borrows an image from country life:

> From the field comes the joy of the harvest,
> From the vine the fruit that gives nourishment,
> From the Scriptures the teaching that gives life.[61]

Ambrose's words are even more charged. He says that when we drink from Sacred Scripture, the life-sap of the eternal Word penetrates the veins of our soul and our inner faculties.[62] Bernard draws a striking parallel between Mary's womb and the hidden depths of the sacred text. He voices his enthusiasm in these words: "Now in the deep womb of the sacred word I will search for myself spirit and life . . .; but that which is concealed within is of the Holy Spirit."[63] It is not, of course, the material sound of the syllables that injects the divine saving power into the soul's veins. If that were the case, the word would be acting by a kind of magic power, like a magician's formula. Even with regard to the words of the sacraments, theology is revising the formulas in order to avoid all appearance of magic, however remote.

It would be foolish to do this to the entire Bible, just when we are rediscovering the fruitfulness of a traditional and very different concept.

The Word acts as a "word." That means it must be understood and accepted. It presupposes openness on the part of the reader. Here all the spiritual dispositions we will mention later come into play, faith being the first of many, indissolubly linked as it is to the word. If hearing the word of Christ gives rise to the first act of faith (Rom 10:17), then faith in turn influences every subsequent hearing of that word. Only faith, animated by love, can create the spiritual atmosphere for the

---

[60] John Chrysostom, *De Statuis*, hom. I (PG 49, 18).

[61] Ephrem, *Opera*, Rome 1743, 41.

[62] Ambrose, *In Ps.* I, 33: "Sacred Scripture is drunk and devoured when the life-sap of the eternal Word penetrates the veins of the spirit and the powers of the soul" (PL 14, 984).

[63] Bernard, *In Cant.*, 73, 2 (PL 183, 1134d).

Word to properly ring out. Then, humbly welcomed, it is planted in our hearts and has the power to save our souls (Jas 1:21). While it enlightens, it also transforms. Even on a human level, the word is the means for creating communion between two minds. When God speaks, he communicates himself, and his communion is grace. We become one spirit with him.

An inexhaustible mystery

"How amazing is the profundity of your words. . . . How amazing their profundity, O my God, how amazingly deep they are!"[64] This cry, wrung from Augustine's heart by Scripture, finds rich echoes in the tradition. Miraculously fruitful, thanks to the presence of that Spirit which Bernard calls a "manifold spirit,"[65] Scripture is an unfathomable world. Its dimensions are as long and wide, as high and deep as the mystery it contains. We may venture there, but we can never say we have reached the bottom.

Our starting point is a concept of Scripture we could call sacramental. Besides the word "sacrament" which appears frequently, there is a whole language which echoes that used to describe the liturgy and the incarnation.[66] As soon as the Word assumed our flesh, Christ became the "primordial sacrament" according to Origen. In him the concept of sacrament is supremely and fully expressed: a material element containing a divine reality. He is the sacrament of the encounter with

---

[64] Augustine, *Conf.* XII, 14, 17.

[65] Bernard, *In Cant.* 47, 4 (PL 183, 1009c).

[66] See H. de Lubac, op.cit., I, 396–408. Especially striking is the frequent parallel made by tradition between Word and Eucharist. A quotation from Jerome (*In Eccles.*, III) can serve as representative: "Since the Lord's flesh is real food and his blood real drink, according to the anagogical sense, our only good in the present age is to eat his flesh and drink his blood, not only in the mystery [of the Eucharist] but also in the reading of Scripture" (PL 23, 1039a). See also *Anecdota Mareds.* (III, 2, 290–91): "The Bread of Christ and his flesh are the word of God and heavenly teaching"; see ibid., 301–2.

God.[67] Those who encountered Jesus of Nazareth encountered the living God. The ecclesial signs we call sacraments continue this dispensation. That is why everything in the liturgy tends to look beyond the signs to the saving presence of Christ. All this is transferred *en bloc* to the Bible. Here, too, there is a material sign, the Word. And this Word—does it not usually present events, that is, realities recorded within the concrete and tangible limits of history? But it is sacred history; the events are salvific. Those material elements mediate the divine; they express and communicate an invisible reality. Here too we must go beyond the external element or wrapping—what the Fathers call "the letter"—in order to reach the "mystery" or hidden sense of Scripture. And always, there is only one mystery, the mystery of Christ.

The Bible and creation

Profound thinker that he was, John Scotus Eriugena reduced these traditional views to a logical and impressive system. A philosopher more than a theologian, he prefers to compare the Bible to creation. Creation is God's first book. Augustine, too, was fascinated by this idea. Using one of his clever word plays, he said that the universe was written by God as a book, and Scripture was made by God as a universe.[68]

Both Scripture and creation, says John Scotus, are reflections of the eternal light.[69] Without sin, creation would have been enough.[70] The world would have been a book, large and clear, and every creature would have been a manifestation of God.[71]

---

[67] This is the title of a now famous book by E. Schillebeeckx, *Christ the Sacrament of the Encounter with God.*

[68] Augustine, *In Ps.* VIII, 7 (CCL 33, 52). Later, an obscure medieval writer would go so far as to say that creation is "like a corporeal and visible gospel": Herbert of Boseham, *Liber melorum* III (PL 190, 1355d).

[69] John Scotus Eriugena, *Hom. in prol. Joann.:* "The eternal light reveals itself to the world in two ways: Scripture and creation" (PL 122, 289c).

[70] Idem, *Super hier. coel.* II, 1 (PL 122, 146c).

[71] Hugh of St. Victor (?), *Miscellanea* lib. I, tit. 63 (PL 177, 505a).

But after sin, it bears a curse which makes it opaque to the divine light. What is more, our mind bears a curse which makes it unclean and unable to understand the language of things, to see in them a reflection of eternal beauty.[72] And so God created a new universe, spreading before us this new firmament which sings his glory: Sacred Scripture. Upon entering it, we can hear his Word again, see his light, enter into communion with him. At the same time we find the key to unlock the book of creation. In the light of the Word, the material universe also becomes transparent again. When combined, the two realities present an identical structure (a sacramental structure to be exact), since they symbolize the divine. On the surface, creation presents a visible aspect and the Bible a literal sense. Therefore the starting point is "the simplicity of the letter and material creation." But we must not stop there. We must go farther to reach, in one case, "the spirit," and in the other, "the reason." This exciting journey leads "to the summit of contemplation."[73] In fact, says John Scotus, whether it is "the surface of Scripture" or "the material forms of the world," both serve to clothe Christ—two veils, as it were, that mask the radiance of his face while at the same time reflecting its beauty.[74]

We have come to the heart of the ancients' idea of the Bible. "Christ is contained in the literal sense" is their constant refrain.[75] All Scripture is a great sacrament. It contains, in a kind

[72] Chrysostom insists on this second theme—the impurity of the human mind after sin—when he writes: "It would have been good if we had not needed the written letter; if, instead of the Scriptures, a pure life would have prepared us to possess the grace of the Spirit. As pages are written with ink, our hearts would have been written by the Spirit. But we lost this grace forever. And so let us spend our time on this second source of riches and busy ourselves with what has been written. Scripture was not given to us only to be preserved in books, but to be kneaded into our hearts. . . .": *In Matt.* hom. I, cited by Ludolph the Carthusian, *Vita Christi*, prol., Paris 1579, f. 4 DE.

[73] John Scotus Eriugena, *In Joann.*, 3 (PL 122, 342–43).

[74] Idem, *De div. nat.* III, 35 (PL 122, 725d). *Super hier. coel.* II (136c). *In Joann.*, I (307b).

[75] Hervé of Bourg-Dieu, *In Cor.* (PL 181, 824c).

of material wrapping, the mystery of salvation whose center is Christ.[76] Guided by the Spirit, I must go beyond the letter to the depths of the mystery where I encounter him.

An immense weight of mysteries

We will now examine this idea more closely. It explains why the ancients felt as they did in the presence of every biblical text. For them it is a mystery whose dimensions are the same as those of the mystery of Christ. It is infinite in extent; no reading can ever reach the bottom. They love to use various images: it is a vast sea,[77] an unfathomable abyss.[78] Augustine speaks of "an immense weight of mysteries."[79] And before him Origen was overcome with fear upon entering the vast, deep and mysterious sea of God's Word with his fragile boat.[80] It is an exploration that will never end. No matter how much the mind reaches out and strives to understand, it can never encompass the full dimensions of a sacred text "that spans infinite mysteries."[81] It is always that way when we are dealing with divine realities. Newman shared this conviction of the Fathers:

> It is in point to notice also the structure and style of Scripture, a structure so unsystematic and various, and a style so figurative and indirect, that no one would presume at first sight to

[76] Augustine, *In Ps.* 30, 2, 9: "Almost everywhere Christ has been foretold by the prophets under the veil of symbols . . ." (PL 36, 245).

[77] Gregory, *In Ezech.* I, 6, 13 (PL 76, 834–35). Ambrose (PL 16, 738, 880 etc.).

[78] Ambrosius Autpertus, *In Apoc.* IX (*Max. Bibl. Vet. Patrum*, XIII, Lyons 1677, 613b); Rupert *In Apoc.* IV, 7 (PL 169, 956d); Honorius, *In Ps.* 32, 7 (PL 193, 1324c); Godfrey of Admont, *Hom.* 12 *in Script.* (PL 174, 1112d).

[79] Augustine, *In Ps.* 143, 1 (CCL 40, 2072).

[80] Origen, *In Gen.* hom. 9–1: "Just as one who goes to sea in a small boat feels extremely anxious about entrusting a small vessel to such huge waves, so we too suffer when we dare to penetrate such a great sea of mysteries" (PG 12, 210).

[81] Irimbert, *In Ruth prol.* (Pez, *Thesaurus*, IV, 444).

say what is in it and what is not. It cannot, as it were, be mapped, or its contents catalogued; but after all our diligence, to the end of our lives and the end of the Church, it must be an unexplored and unsubdued land, with heights and valleys, forests and streams, on the right and left of our path and close about us, full of concealed wonders and choice treasures.[82]

There is a radical disproportion between human beings and the mystery of the Word that was written for them.[83] "Who has enough spiritual understanding to explain these mysteries?" wondered Origen.

Here tradition is only a continuation of the reflections on the great mystery of the Law found in Israel's wisdom literature:

> It overflows like the Pishon, with wisdom,
>   and like the Tigris at the time of the first fruits.
> It runs over, like the Euphrates, with understanding,
>   and like the Jordan at harvest time.
> It pours forth instruction like the Nile,
>   like the Gihon at the time of vintage.
> The first man did not know wisdom fully,
>   nor will the last one fathom her.
> For her thoughts are more abundant than the sea,
>   and her counsel deeper than the great abyss (Sir 24:25-29).

---

[82] *Essay on the Development of Christian Doctrine* II, 1, 14. The text is cited by H. de Lubac, op.cit., I, 126, where we have borrowed numerous other references for this section. It should be noted that their faith in the Bible's mysterious nature led the ancients to accept various explanations of the same text—a multiplicity justified in their eyes by its inexhaustible riches. The eclectic nature of many medieval commentaries, including those of John Scotus Eriugena, seems to be based on this conviction. While their faith insight as to the Bible's "mystery" remains valid and fruitful, we obviously cannot follow their procedure which, under the pretext of analyzing every possibility of the text, lends itself to a kind of exegetical relativism. Every biblical text has but one sense, even if that one sense can be understood on various levels.

[83] Gregory, *In Reg.*, proem. 1, 3: "Since it is divinely inspired, Sacred Scripture is as superior to the most gifted geniuses as these endowed persons are inferior to God. For they see nothing in its spiritual depths except what God in his goodness is pleased to reveal to them. Therefore no one is so proficient in the knowledge of Scripture that he cannot advance

This statement leaves us humbled before the Word, but it does not deter our search. In fact it encourages us. There is always something left to discover; we can always draw new water from this bottomless well.[84] At every reading, it is as if there were a new world to discover.[85] It is as if God "had already begun anew, as it were, to open to us that very great abyss of mysteries." These are the words of the Cistercian Aelred of Rievaulx.[86] His confrere Gilbert of Hoyland echoes him: "New things can always be discovered in Christ. Into the new, one may penetrate."[87]

Once again it is Gregory who finds the most apt terms for describing this faith insight. He says that Scripture grows with the mind of the reader:

> The divine words grow with the one who reads them. . . . Where the mind of the reader is directed, there, too, the sacred text ascends; for . . . it grows with us, it rises with us.[88]

These words are justly famous and widely repeated in later tradition.[89] What exactly do they mean? Gregory points us in the right direction, saying that when the reader addresses a question to the text, the answer is in proportion to the reader's maturity.[90]

---

further, since all human progress is always subject to the inspiration of the Most High" (PL 79, 19d).

[84] Just how familiar was this image of the well can be seen from the rich documentation given by H. de Lubac, op.cit., I, 126.

[85] Smaragdus, *Diad. monac.*, c. III: "It often happens that the soul, enkindled by the grace of heavenly contemplation, is snatched up to heavenly things. Then it realizes that the words of Scripture are full of mystical meanings. . . . Sacred Scripture grows in some way with those who read it. Beginners investigate it, as it were, but to experts it is revealed as ever new" (PL 102, 598ab).

[86] Aelred of Rievaulx, *De oner.*, serm. XIII (PL 195, 405c).

[87] Gilbert of Hoyland, *In Cant.* 14, 1 (PL 184, 68c).

[88] Gregory, *In Ezech.* I, 8 (PL 76, 843–44).

[89] Rabanus Maurus, Isidore, Defensor of Ligugé, etc., reproduce these texts of Gregory in their compilations.

[90] Gregory, *In Ezech.* I, 7 (PL 76, 847). He wrote: "Have you reached the active life? It [Scripture] goes with you. Have you attained detachment

The objective dimensions of the Word do not grow; they already correspond to the mystery of Christ. Its lifegiving power is unlimited, thanks to the presence of the Spirit. It is the reader's mind that grows. And it grows through the influence of that Word, which creates in the soul of the faithful reader an ever-new capacity to receive it.[91] Clothed with the light of God, the mind reaches out.[92] And to the extent that the receiver's mind reaches out, so too does the Word. John Cassian expressed this in categorical terms:

> As our mind is increasingly renewed by this study, Scripture begins to take on a new face. A mysteriously deeper sense of it comes to us and somehow the beauty of it stands out more and more as we get farther into it.[93]

"The higher you rise," says Rabanus Maurus, "the higher the divine Word rises with you."[94] And as we advance, we can obviously never say, "This is enough." Gregory has been called the Doctor of Desire[95] because his spirituality demands continuous self-transcendence. One who is spiritual soars to God, tirelessly, on eagle's wings. Time becomes a providential means for opening ourselves more and more to his "infinite fullness,"[96] to the "unlimited light"[97] of his Word which reveals the very mystery of God.

---

and constancy of spirit? It stands with you. Have you arrived at the contemplative life by the grace of God? It flies with you."

[91] Here is Origen's careful description of the constant spiritual renewal produced by contact with Scripture: "Our soul is renewed by a life in accord with wisdom, meditation on the Word of God, and spiritual understanding of his law. If we advance each day by the reading of Scripture and our [spiritual] understanding becomes more acute, then we are constantly new, day after day" *In Rom.* IX, 1 (PG 14, 1206).

[92] Gregory, *In Ezech.* II, 5 n. 17 (PL 76, 995b).

[93] Cassian, *Coll.* XIV, c. 11 (*Sourc. chrét.* 54, p. 197). [English tr. Colm Luibheid - CWS].

[94] Rabanus Maurus, *In Ezech.* II (PL 110, 534d).

[95] See J. Leclercq, *L'amour des lettres et le désire de Dieu*, op.cit., 30–39.

[96] Gregory, *Moral.* 26, 34 (PL 76, 369).

[97] Idem, *Moral.* 10, 13 (PL 75, 928).

How amazing is the mystery of a living Word that grows through the spiritual experience of a person of faith. Or the other way around, and more exactly: how amazing is the mystery of a life of faith which is enriched through an ever deeper experience of the Word of life, and which is renewed as it constantly advances. The council texts could not ignore such a fertile concept; it is expressed in n. 8 of *Dei Verbum*.[98] Growth involves three things: the contemplative activity of believers who, like Mary, ponder the Word; the experience of spiritual realities that enables them to look with more penetrating eyes upon the Word; and finally, preaching. Note the order: contemplation and experience come first. The humus in which the seed of the Word takes root is *life*, not ministry—not even an official ministry such as that of the hierarchy.[99] The final goal of this growth is the fullness of truth: "Thus, as the centuries go by, the church is always advancing towards the plenitude of divine truth, until eventually the words of God are fulfilled in it" (DV 8).This fulfillment is sacred history's final goal. Only when the kingdom of Christ has achieved its full dimensions and God is "all in all" will the mystery of the Word be fully revealed and actualized.

[98] "There is a growth in insight into the realities and words that are being passed on. This comes about through the contemplation and study of believers who ponder these things in their hearts (see Luke 2:19 and 51). It comes from the intimate sense of spiritual realities which they experience. And it comes from the preaching of those who, on succeeding to the office of bishop, have received the sure charism of truth. Thus, as the centuries go by, the church is always advancing towards the plenitude of divine truth, until eventually the words of God are fulfilled in it" (DV 8).

[99] Obviously it is not a question of relegating the office of bishop to second place with respect to the Word. It is part of the Church's essential structure, and many conciliar texts emphasize this. See the small volume entitled *La Parola di Dio e il Concilio* (Temi conciliari, 4), Milan 1968, where we have shown this. It is simply a question of stressing that growth in understanding takes place through an experience which belongs to all the people of God, hierarchy and faithful, and which then flows back into preaching.

The divine Exegete[100]

We must not think that the agent of growth is human beings and their subjective efforts to understand. The human mind is too limited to understand a Word that comes from a place far above human intelligence. The agent of growth is the Spirit of Christ who animates the Church from within and spurs it on. It is he who "leads believers to the full truth, causing the Word of Christ to dwell in them in all its richness."[101] He alone can open the eyes of our soul. Jerome said that we cannot understand Scripture without the help of the Spirit who inspired it.[102] "The soul reaches out to understand Scripture through the anointing of the Spirit who reveals its mystery."[103]

The ancients saw this foreshadowed in the action of Christ who took bread in his hand, blessed and broke it. In every tradition, the bread of the sacrament recalls the bread of the Word.[104] Christ's act is repeated in the Church "not only in the mystery of the Eucharist, but also in the reading of Scripture," as Rupert says.[105] He "breaks this bread, shares this Word," and the result is "the knowledge of Scripture."[106] It was this gesture that opened the eyes of the disciples at Emmaus. They recognized Christ and at the same time understood the Scriptures: "Then he opened their minds to understand the scriptures."[107]

---

[100] Gregory says: "He who is author of the Holy Testaments is himself also their Exegete" *In Ezech.* I, 7, 17 (PL 76, 848d).

[101] DV 8.

[102] Jerome, *Epist.* 120, c. 10 (PL 22, 997).

[103] Henry of Marcy, *De per. civ. Dei*, tr. 16 (PL 204, 384d).

[104] This classic theme is found in a well-known chapter of the *Imitation of Christ* (Bk. IV, ch. 11). Pope John, with his persuasive style, used it in a Holy Thursday homily, and the council refers to it at least twice: DV 21 and AGD 6.

[105] Rupert, *In Eccles.* (PL 168, 1230–31).

[106] Ambrose, *In Luc.* VI, 91 (*Sourc. chrét.* 45, 262; n. 63, 250); Honorius, *Sp. Eccl.*, (PL 172, 895c) etc.

[107] The medieval monks were very fond of this verse; it gave them an unusually rich spiritual vocabulary to describe the work of grace within the soul, opening it to the light of the Word. See M. Magrassi, *La Bibbia nei chiostri da Cluny a Citeaux*, in *Bibbia e spiritualità*, Rome 1967, 211–15.

Only the sovereign working of his grace can produce such understanding; exegetical acumen or learning are not involved. This is the all-powerful act of Christ who "speaks to our heart and guides us into all truth through his Spirit."[108] Origen would say: ". . . as Jesus recites the law to you and reveals to your hearts its spiritual understanding. . . ."[109] He alone can break the external wrapping of his Word and reveal its spiritual sense so that we can penetrate the depths where lie the secrets of God.

As we end this section, the cry we alluded to at the beginning becomes loud and clear. In it, Augustine sums up his experience of the Word:

> How amazing is the profundity of your words! We are confronted with a superficial meaning that offers easy access to the unlettered; yet how amazing their profundity, O my God, how amazingly deep they are! To look into that depth makes me shudder, but it is the shudder of awe, the trembling of love.

Similarly, the words of Chrysostom: "Even if the phrase is short, its power is great. Often, one word taken from there is enough to serve as viaticum for an entire lifetime."[110]

And when the mystery is unveiled, it is Christ who is revealed. The passage that leads to the understanding of Scripture leads to life in Christ.[111] When the Scriptures are opened, he admits us to his private domain. Every deeper reading of the text is a movement toward him. The essential task of exegesis, as one Cistercian says, is to apply everything to the mystery of Christ.[112] In an even more packed expression, Ignatius of Antioch said that we must go to Scripture as to the flesh of Christ.[113] He is the one center where all the lines of the biblical universe meet. And if it is true that every sentence of Scripture, since it contains an unfathomable mystery, has many

---

[108] Rupert, *In Oseam,* lib. I (PL 168, 47cd).
[109] Origen, *In Jos.,* hom. 9, n. 9 (PG 12, 878).
[110] John Chrysostom, *De statuis,* hom. I (PG 49, 18).
[111] Othloh, *De cursu spir.* c. 20 (PL 146, 213a).
[112] Gilbert of Hoyland, *In Cant.* 30, 5 (PL 184, 157c).
[113] Ignatius of Antioch, *Ad Philad.* 4, 1.

senses, it is even more true that every sentence of Scripture always has only one sense.[114]

This one book is Christ

This is the fundamental insight of all the ancients. Following St. Paul, they saw the Old Testament as a learning period leading to Christ. It is a story that finds its decisive turning point in him; it is a Word that is summed up in him and becomes a person; it is a revelation that achieves full clarity in him.

The Bible is both revelation and history. Playing on these words, someone has said that it is the history of revelation and the revelation of history. In any case, the two ideas are closely connected, because the Word of God is creative. It creates the event and moves the course of history ahead, at the same time shedding light on its salvific meaning. Gregory says this concisely the *Moralia:* "With the same words it tells a story and reveals a mystery."

The two realities meet and are supremely actualized in Christ. He is the final realization of what God intended to do; he is the final expression of what God intended to say. In the mystery of Christ, all the themes of salvation history converge, and the entire message of revelation is summed up: "A short Word, a concise Word."[115]

Recapitulation of salvation history

Early tradition enthusiastically tried to explain these two things. First of all, Christ is the fulfillment of the divine plan.

---

[114] See L. Bouyer, *Le sens de la vie monastique,* Paris 1950, 270–71.

[115] Bernard, *In Cant.* serm. 59, n. 9: "O Word abridged, yet living and powerful" (PL 183, 1065d); Aelred of Rievaulx, *De Jesu duod.,* n. 13: "Jesus was an abbreviated Word but an effective one bringing consummation to earth, summing up the Law and the Prophets in the twofold commandment of love" (PL 184, 857c); cf. *Spec. charit.,* I, 16: "O Word that consummates and rightly abridges! Word of charity, Word of love, Word of predilection, Word of all perfection" (PL 195, 520a).

No one said it better than Irenaeus: "He recapitulated in himself the long history of humankind and procured for us a
'short cut' to salvation."[116] He recapitulates the divine plan because he finalizes it from beginning to end. This radical chris-
tological orientation lies within the entire Old Testament. It
was not imposed from without, like a label, by Christian
apologetics: "It is within it and penetrates all its parts."[117] If we
represent salvation history by a line, Christ is at its end,
middle, and every point in between.[118]

This fundamental insight, which is the true heart of all traditional exegesis, is very impressive. Thanks to it, we are witnesses of the great central event as it advances relentlessly,
looms and becomes a crescendo: from the first verse of Genesis to the last verse of the Apocalypse, where Christ appears as
the Alpha and the Omega, the first and the last, the beginning
and the end. He is the keystone who gives a single meaning to
all the events of history, blending them into perfect unity.

All the elements that make up this divine plan are signs that
proclaim its mysterious coming. They also effect its mysterious presence.[119] The Old Testament is not only an external
preparation for the mystery of Christ; it is already an integral
part of it. Israel already lives it and is aware of it—although
imperfectly—thanks to the prophetic revelation, which points
with increasing clarity to the *eschaton* at the end of time. His
mystery is already at work in the People of God and their institutions, which prepare hearts to receive him[120] and fore-
shadow his redeeming work. It is already at work in the
history of Israel, which from its beginning is determined by its

---

[116] Irenaeus, *Advers. haer.*, III, 18, 1 (PG 7, 832b).

[117] Hoskyns, *Mysterium salutis,* cited in H. de Lubac, op.cit., II–I, 196.

[118] O. Cullman develops this idea in his great work *Christ and Time.*

[119] See P. Grelot, *Sens chrétien de l'Ancien Testament* (Bibliothèque de
Théologie, ser. I, 3), Paris 1962, 159–65. He tries to specify the manner of
Christ's mysterious presence in the realities of the Old Testament. Although the entire work is in line with modern scientific studies, it is permeated with the classic insights of the Fathers. It would be of great
interest to anyone who would like to begin serious study of the Bible.

[120] Ibid., 196–209.

end, and whose biblical figures present a mysterious sketch of it.[121] As the mystery is gradually revealed, Israel experiences it under the veil of institutions and figurative events. Christ gives life to all these things from within. He draws them along toward his coming like a powerful river current that irresistibly sweeps everything in its direction.

Using another image, we can say that these things are already secretly pregnant with his mystery, like an ear of grain that swells in expectation of the mature fruit. Rupert sees the Old Testament Church, "spiritually pregnant in the prophets," advance through time bearing the eternal Word in its womb.[122] All history is seen as a pregnancy that leads essentially to the birth of the incarnate Word of God. That moment marks the fullness of time. Then Israel's partial experience yields to the experience of the Word of life—heard, seen, and touched by his witnesses (1 John 1:1-2). And it continues sacramentally in the history of the Church, so much so that Ambrose could say: "You have shown yourself to me face to face, O Christ. I encounter you in your sacraments." Meanwhile history moves toward its final end: Christ's glorious return at the end of time, when the mystery of salvation will be accomplished and we will enter with him into glory.

These insights—briefly sketched here—are the substance of patristic and medieval theology and exegesis. Their expression is unequalled. Everything in the Bible is regarded as a sign. The words "Unto the end" occur in the title of one of the psalms. Augustine notes: "When you hear the psalm say *Unto the end,* your heart should turn to Christ."[123] He is the end beyond which there is nothing more to seek. The unity of Scripture is based on him, its one and only object. In the famous statement of Hugh of St. Victor: "All Sacred Scripture is but one book, and this one book is Christ; because all Sacred Scrip-

[121] Ibid., 275–326.

[122] See M. Magrassi, *Teologia e storia nel pensiero di Ruperto di Deutz,* Rome 1959, 160ff.

[123] Augustine, *In Ps.* 139, 3 (CCL 40, 2013). See Cassiodorus, *In psalt.* praef., c. III (PL 70, 14–15); Cyril of Alexandria, *De adoratione in spiritu,* 10 (PG 68, 700cd).

ture speaks of Christ, and all Sacred Scripture is fulfilled in Christ."[124] From the "totality of Scripture" he forms the one Word of God.[125] The ancients never tire of commenting on the text where Paul, referring to his fellow Jews, speaks of "a veil over their faces" (2 Cor 3:12ff). To read the Bible and not find Christ in it is like having a heavy veil before our eyes: we see nothing.

Such is the marvelous pedagogy of a God who, through successive stages, "finally leads his people into the presence of Someone."[126] There they are left, for after him there is really nothing new. He is newness, complete and lasting: "He brought all newness when he brought himself."[127] He sums up the divine plan; he is the "Amen" to all of God's promises (see 2 Cor 1:19); he is the "universal recapitulation" who brings all things to fulfillment.[128]

A concentration of light: "The shortest Word"

In recapitulating the divine plan Christ also recapitulates and sums up the Word that creates its course and sheds light on its meaning. The "many words" become forever "the one Word."[129] In the past God's Word was fragmented into many

[124] Hugh of St. Victor, *De arca Noe mor.,* II, 8 (PL 176, 642c).

[125] See Rupert, *De Trin., De op. S. Spir.,* I, 6: "The totality of Scripture is the one Word of God. . . . And so when we read Sacred Scripture, we are handling the Word of God; the Son of God is before our eyes as in a mirror, indistinctly" (PL 167, 1575).

[126] This apt expression comes from C. Hauret, *Comment lire la Bible? La table ronde,* November 1956, 141.

[127] Irenaeus, *Advers haer.* IV, 34, 1 (PG 7, 1083b).

[128] Adam of St. Victor, sequence "Zyma vetus expurgetur," vv. 19-21 (in L. Gautier, *Oeuvres poétiques d'Adam de Saint Victor,* 3rd ed. 1894, 47): "The Law is a shadow of the things to come: / Christ, the end of the promises, / Who brings all things to fulfillment."

[129] Rupert, *In Joann.,* lib. VII: "For the many words he has spoken are one word, the one Word who himself became flesh. God has placed this one Word on the lips of our souls through many words, that is, through many simple and distinct sounds, through many mysteries: his incarnation, birth, resurrection and ascension" (PL 169, 494c).

human words. It rang out in many ways, all of them partial, through the hearts and mouths of many sacred writers (Heb 1:1-2). To be sure, God in his mystery speaks but one eternal Word in his permanent act of begetting the Logos: "God has spoken only once."[130] But as heard by humans, it is manifold; it spreads through the varied and fragmentary language of Scripture.[131] But the time comes for the Word to return to its original unity, when the Word of God pitches his tent among us.[132] In the past, it rang out in the mouths of more-or-less defective human instruments. But now God himself speaks through a human nature assumed in the unity of his person: "Earlier times were granted the prophets who were inspired and filled with the Word of God; we have been granted the Word of God himself as prophet."[133]

At that moment, all the previous words scattered in the Bible through centuries of waiting are gathered into him. They are illuminated, they reveal their ultimate meaning, and they find their center of unity in him. Indeed they always contained the one Word who was expressing himself and secretly directing all things in view of his final appearance.[134] This one Word, which now rings out on the lips of Christ, is (as Origen would say) "the Word that concludes and abbreviates."[135] It condenses all of Scripture into a "summary that brings salvation."[136] It is the "shortest Word" in which all the light is

[130] Bernard, *De div.*, serm. 73 (PL 183, 695b).

[131] Origen, *In Gen.* hom. 14, n. 1: "Although one in his [divine] nature, our Lord Jesus Christ, who is indeed the Son of God, appears to us manifold and varied in the figures and images of the Scriptures" (PG 12, 236). Augustine, *In Ps.* 103, s. IV, 1: "The one Word of God has spread itself through all Scripture and echoes on the lips of the saints. . . ." (CCL 40, 1521).

[132] Augustine, *In Ps.* 61, n. 18 (CCL 39, 786).

[133] Idem, *In Joann.*, 24, 7 (PL 35, 1596).

[134] See J. Daniélou, *Message évangélique et culture ellénistique*, 317–53; H. de Lubac, *Histoire et esprit*, Paris 1950, 260ff, 336–46.

[135] This term, which was to undergo much development, especially in the Cistercian school (see note 160), originates with Origen, *In Rom.*, VII, 19 (PG 14, 1153–54). *In Luc.*, hom. 34 (PG 13, 1886–88).

[136] Bernard, *De diligendo Deo*, VII, 21 (PL 182, 986).

concentrated,[137] in which we can clearly perceive "the very marrow of Scripture."[138] But while human language in striving for brevity often becomes obscure,[139] here it is the opposite: the divine Word, when abbreviated, becomes supremely clear.[140]

In condensing all things into Christ, Scripture is not impoverished. Instead its soul is revealed, its innermost recesses are opened and it is transfigured. In it, says Paul Claudel, "the Word is spread before us and there we can read it at first sight."[141] This is the constant of Christian exegesis through the ages. Climates change and exegetical methods are refined, but the believer who reads the Bible with faith always finds only Christ there. That was how he himself read it:

> From all its elements he creates a divine synthesis, not from without but from within. He shines his inner light on the prophecies; they are reunited, they lose all trace of the circumstances in which they were spoken, they are harmonized and perfected. . . . Opening the Bible, Jesus sees in it the reflection of the light that shines within him; he hears in it a faint echo of the Word that echoes in his human consciousness.[142]

But the "shortest Word" adds to its luminous density an astonishing concreteness. The message cannot be separated from the person, and that Person is the incarnate Word. At first, the Word was only "audible," but now it is also "visible and tangible." No longer is it "written and silent" but "incarnate and living."[143] The ancients created a wonderful and endless series of variations on this theme,[144] which is also echoed in later authors such as Olier.[145]

[137] Absalon, *Serm.* 22 (PL 211, 130c).
[138] Rupert, *In Joann.*, lib. VI (PL 169, 441d).
[139] See Horace, *Ars poetica*, 25–26.
[140] Garnerius of Rochefort, *Serm. 5 de nativ. Dom.* (PL 205, 599c).
[141] P. Claudel, *Un poète regarde la Croix*, 61.
[142] Text by L. Richard, cited in H. de Lubac, op.cit., II–I, 196.
[143] Bernard, *Super missus est*, hom. 4, n. 11 (PL 183, 86b).
[144] See the section devoted to this in H. de Lubac, op.cit., II–I, 181–97.
[145] *Ufficio della vita interiore di Maria*, Rome 1866, II, 430: "The Mother of Christ, by her word, caused the Word of the Father to become flesh; thus

The supreme revelation

Christ fulfills Scripture, recapitulates the divine plan, and condenses in himself the Word. With that he offers us its supreme revelation. By summarizing it, he reveals its ultimate meaning. He, the one object of exegesis, is also its subject. He is the Book that opens itself.[146] His whole life is exegesis "in act," especially that supreme moment of his life, the paschal mystery. His cross is the key that opens all mysteries.[147] It is the great open book in which all can now read the divine plan. Without that open side from which flowed the springs of the New Testament, "all of us would still be thirsty for the Word of God."[148] Rupert said: "We would not understand the Scriptures if they had not been fulfilled in him."[149]

At that supreme moment, the veil which concealed the mystery of grace was torn,[150] and our inner eyes were opened that we might contemplate it.[151]

> There it is, the turned page that sheds light on everything, like that great illustrated page in the missal. . . . There it is, resplendent and painted red, the great page dividing the two Testaments. All doors are opened at once, all differences vanish, all contradictions are resolved.[152]

---

the Word grows smaller, and if the senses fail to form the Son, the Mother's faith suffices."

[146] Bernard, *In dies Paschae,* serm. 7, n. 12: "Worthy is the Lamb that was slain, worthy is the Lion that has risen—and finally, worthy is the Book to open itself" (PL 183, 280c).

[147] Augustine, *In Ps.* 45, n. 1: "The Lord's cross was a key, for it opened what had been shut" (CCL 38, 518); see *Serm.* 300, n. 3 (PL 39, 1378).

[148] Origen, *In Ex.,* hom. 11, n. 2 (PG 12, 376).

[149] Rupert, *In Joann.,* lib. VI (PL 169, 443bd).

[150] Augustine, *De spir. et litt.,* cap. 15: The Old Testament was "the time when grace had to remain hidden, whereas in the New Testament the passion of Christ had to reveal it by tearing the veil [of the Temple]" (PL 44, 218). See *Serm.* 300, n. 4 (PL 39, 1378). A. Pelletier, in *Rech. de sc. relig.* 46 (1958) 161–80.

[151] Gregory, *Moral.,* XXIX, 14, 26: "By his death, he opened the eyes of our soul . . ." (PL 76, 491a).

[152] P. Claudel, *L'épée et le miroir,* 74.

The seals fall from the Book[153] and revelation attains its full-ness. In its definitive light there appears "the entire mystery of our redemption that was hidden in the books of the Old Testament: unveiled in the Cross and completely fulfilled."[154] It appears in the very act in which it is fulfilled (Eph 3:8-11), an act in which God manifests completely the mystery of his *agape*.

That act effects a real change in Scripture, which the ancients compare to the eucharistic consecration. They love to see Scripture as a loaf of bread in Christ's hands: "The Lord Jesus took the loaves of Scripture in his hands. . . ." In his very act of offering himself to the Father in sacrifice, the bread is consecrated and changed into him.[155] And it is offered: "This Word is . . . the whole Bible in substance in order that we might make of it a single mouthful."[156] Hugh was right to say that "this one book is Christ." He is the Book,[157] the Father's living Word to which every other word bears witness. And de Lubac was also right to say that "Christianity is not the religion of the Bible but the religion of Jesus Christ."[158]

In search of the Beloved

All of this has consequences for *lectio divina*. It is not so much a matter of reading a book as of seeking Someone: "With all its ardor, the Church seeks in Scripture the One whom she loves."[159] Exegesis is not technique; it is mysticism.[160] The mean-

---

[153] Gregory, *In Ezech.*, II, 4, 19 (PL 76, 984a). Caesarius of Arles, *In Apoc.* (Opera omnia [Morin], II, 222). Absalon, *Serm.* 25: "In the passion that book was opened. Eternal power and divinity, hidden from us, began to manifest itself" (PL 211, 150).

[154] Helinandus, *Serm.* 10 (PL 212, 567b).

[155] See Rupert, *In Joann.*, lib. VI (PL 169, 443d).

[156] *Paul Claudel interroge l'Apocalypse*, 50.

[157] Absalon, *Serm.* 25: "The book we have recalled is Christ, of whom it is written in the Apocalypse: *I saw in the right hand of the one seated on the throne a book written within and without.* . . ." (PL 211, 148d).

[158] H. de Lubac, op.cit., II–I, 197.

[159] Honorius, *In Cant.* (PL 172, 447d).

[160] Here is how the task of exegesis is seen by the Cistercian Gilbert of Hoyland, *In Cant.*, XIV, 1: "Hold fast what you hold, and touch linger-

ing of Scripture is not an impersonal truth but the fascinating figure of Christ: "The meaning of Christ, mysterious and hidden."[161] The whole science of exegesis is the ability to recognize Christ.[162] And when great saints such as Origen, Gregory, or Bernard pore over the text, their exegesis becomes an ardent search, a joyful and almost dreamlike discovery, a poem of love.

The Canticle especially provides an opportunity for this. Origen sees Christ behind the wall of the "letter." He sees him peering through the lattices and exclaims: "Behold, the Bridegroom!"[163] True, that joyful cry is often preceded by moments of anxiety. At first the soul grapples with the riddles of the text. To be sure, love for the Word has drawn it, but in the Word it is "Christ whom it longs to drink," like a thirsty deer that longs for running water,[164] yet it cannot find him. But then the darkness clears before the light of spiritual understanding, and the soul "hears from on high the sound of his voice." It hears him coming and, startled, catches sight of him at last "leaping across the mountains, skipping over the hills."[165] And there in the heart of Scripture—what Origen calls the "spiritual sense"—comes the encounter. It is Jesus who appears,[166] leads the soul into his bridal chamber, engages it in intimate conversation, and reveals to it the ineffable mystery of his person:[167] "What eye has not seen, ear has not heard, nor has it ever entered the human heart."

---

ingly and lovingly the word of life. Unroll the scroll of life, the scroll which Jesus unrolls or, rather, which is Jesus himself. Wrap yourself in him. . . . Put on your Beloved, our Lord Jesus Christ . . . for his word is a flame. Herein repose" (PL 184, 68). (English tr. Lawrence C. Braceland).

[161] Origen, *In Cant.*, lib. 1, n. 1 (PG 13, 83).

[162] Paschasius, *In Lam.*, lib. II: "Let knowledge of Scripture be this life; through it Christ is recognized and eternal [life] is prepared for those who believe" (PL 120, 1105a).

[163] Origen, *In Cant.*, lib. 2, n. 10 (*Sourc. chrét.*, 37, 97).

[164] Idem, *In Jer.*, hom. 18, n. 9 (PG 13, 482ab).

[165] Idem, *In Cant.*, 3 (PG 13, 145–84).

[166] Idem, *In Jer.*, hom. 18, n. 10 (PG 13, 484b).

[167] Idem, *In Cant.*, lib. 1, n. 1 (PG 13, 83).

These pages would leave an indelible mark on tradition. St.
Ambrose, in his meditation on Scripture, also hears the sound
of that voice. A mysterious spiritual sense detects the perfume
of his presence, hears the sound of his breathing: "It perceives
the perfume of his presence and says: *Behold, him whom I seek;
behold, him whom I desire.*"[168]

Despite Jerome's more erudite and literary concept of exegesis (its first concern being the *haebraica veritas*), his biblical
commentaries are also heir to this spirit. Gorge says of him: "A
perfume of mystical poetry issues from a similar concept of
exegesis. There is something sanctifying about this immediate
contact with Scripture, about this ascent to God so devoutly
begun."[169]

Among the Cistercians, the Canticle was an obligatory subject and practically a badge of the school. There the inspiration
of Origen, "the mystical exegete,"[170] would continue and be
recreated, as it were, from the *novitas* of Citeaux.[171] It was a
kind of new spring for exegesis. The Canticle's themes were
systematically subjected to spiritual exegesis. Gilbert of Hoyland sees the bride's search for her Beloved as foreshadowing
the soul's search for Christ through meditation on Scripture.[172]
But the Cistercians did not have a monopoly. Rupert had said
earlier: "What does it mean to lay hold of the Beloved if not to
find the meaning of Christ in the Scriptures?"[173] William
Firmat says it even better: "As soon as you have left your
books behind, you have found him whom your soul loves."[174]

---

[168] Ambrose, *In Ps.* 118, *Serm.* 6, n. 6–9 (PL 15, 1269–74; the passage cited
is in 1270c).

[169] D. Gorge, La *"lectio divina" des origines du cénobitisme à Saint Benoît et
Cassiodore*, vol. I: *Saint Jérôme et la lecture sacrée dans le milieu ascétique ro-
main*, Paris 1925, 190–91.

[170] E. Gilson, *La Théologie mystique de Saint Bernard*, Paris 1947, 28.

[171] Hugh of Mettelus, *Epist. ad s. Bern.* (PL 182, 687–88).

[172] Gilbert of Hoyland, *In Cant., serm.* 4, n. 8–9 (PL 184, 31–32).

[173] Rupert, *In Zach.* lib. III (PL 168, 749c).

[174] William Firmat, *Exhortatio in amorem claustri et desiderium lectionis
divinae* (ed. Leclercq, *Anal. monast.* II, 36): "Run here and there, hurry, turn
around, turn back again, search the Scriptures and ransack the library, if
necessary, if only to find Wisdom. . . ."

A monk from the Abbey of Admont goes still further. He feels himself a sharer in the privilege of John, who rested his head on Christ's heart at the Last Supper. The equivalence on which this idea is based is revealing: "Sacred Scripture is the breast of Jesus."[175]

It is Bernard, of course, who develops the theme more coherently and with a stronger mystical thrust. One feels that the texts are not stating theory but are rooted in experience. "The thirsty soul," he says, "eagerly prolongs its contact with Scripture, certain to find there the One for whom it thirsts."[176] As it strives to search the mysteries of Scripture, its feels aglow with divine love. An infusion of light from the Bridegroom illuminates the intellect, and there is an extraordinary expansion of the mind.[177] These are irrefutable signs of his presence. The Beloved is coming to meet the soul:

> If I feel that my eyes are opened to understand the Scriptures, so that I am enlightened from above to preach the word of wisdom from the heart or reveal the mysteries of God . . . I have no doubt that the Bridegroom is with me.[178]

Note the equivalence. This is how the Lord leads the soul to intimacy with him. Garden, wine-cellar, and bridal chamber represent the three successive stages of intimacy and correspond to the three senses of Scripture: historical, moral, mystical.[179]

This experience of Christ in the Scriptures is not, of course, constant; the "visits" of the Word are intermittent. After revealing himself, he often hides. Bernard calls this "a divine game."[180] The soul alternates between light and darkness, joy and anguish. Alternation is one of Bernard's favorite themes: "The Word comes and goes."[181] When he is absent, we wait

---

[175] Godfrey of Admont, *Hom. dom.* 51 (PL 174, 339b).

[176] Bernard, *In Cant.*, serm. 23, n. 3 (PL 183, 885d).

[177] Idem, *In Cant.*, serm. 57, n. 7–8 (1053–54).

[178] Idem, *In Cant.*, serm. 69, n. 6 (1115b).

[179] Idem, *In Cant.*, serm. 23, n. 3 (885d); *De div.*, serm. 92, 2 (PL 183, 714b).

[180] Idem, *In Cant.*, serm. 74, n. 1–7 (1149–52).

[181] Idem, *In Cant.*, serm. 74, n. 4 (1140–42).

with patient desire for his return. This alternation is part of every true religious experience. "If then," notes de Lubac, "the exegesis of St. Bernard is unquestionably the exegesis of a mystic, it is no less true that . . . by its very structure it is the mysticism of an exegete."[182] And this can be said of a whole generation of monks. Having devoted their lives to seeking and loving Christ, they were able, through the pages of the sacred Book, to have a living encounter with him.

Later, a slow divorce began to take place between piety and exegesis. Eventually it was finalized. A violent separation took place between two realities that had been joined together by God, since the word of God is a Word of life. We are still feeling the effects of all this. Is it not time to re-establish unity? Are not all the necessary conditions to be found in the Church today? Surely it would be helpful, in doing this, to return to the rich sources from which we have unearthed a few fragments here, not out of scholarly curiosity, but by way of vital rediscovery. It is an amazing experience that can still serve as a model today. It can be the stimulus and animating force behind our reading, which is so proud of its scientific tools but so lacking in spiritual power.

[182] H. de Lubac, op.cit., I, 599.

⊹⊨ 4 ⊨⊹

Lectio Divina: Concrete Dispositions

We have given a quick summary of the faith insights that guided our ancestors in their reading of the Bible. More than once this has led us to emphasize some aspect of their particular method of reading. Now we must look at this more closely.

This chapter attempts to answer a question that could be put thus: If the Bible is all these things, what spiritual dispositions do we need when we read it? These dispositions flow from a series of adjectives describing this "prayed reading": diligent, sapiential, dialogical, committed. Before devoting a separate section to each disposition, it would be well to mention the ascetical dispositions that serve as remote preparation for reading.

Ascetical dispositions

Purity of heart

The ancients gave special attention to the moral dispositions that make us receptive to the Word, like the good ground in the gospel parable of the sower. First, we need a deep ascetical commitment. Its object is purity of heart or soul. As used by the ancients, this expression refers to the absence of all love of creatures that might distract us from love of God and aware-

ness of God's presence. It means total freedom to be totally
dedicated to the love of God. It is practiced in the face of external attractions (the world and the devil) and internal pas-
sions (disordered inclinations of the senses, thoughts, and
movements of the will). In this way it arrives at "interior re-
nunciation of evil habits."[1] From a heart that has attained interior purity, pure prayer may arise (*Rule of St. Benedict*, chap.
20). This disposition influences all understanding of the divine: "Truth does not reveal itself to the impure; wisdom does
not entrust itself to such."[2]

We know how important this theme became in Western monastic tradition. Our source is Cassian, who offers us an extra-
ordinarily rich text. If we meditate on it, it can pierce our soul
like a sword. The text is from *Conference XIV*, which deals with
spiritual knowledge. For Cassian, as for all the ancients, this
meant concrete knowledge of Scripture:

> For it is one thing to be a skilled talker and a shining speaker.
> It is something else to enter into the very heart and core of
> heavenly utterances, to contemplate with heart's purest gaze
> the deep and hidden mysteries. This is not something to be
> possessed by humanistic lore and worldly erudition. It will be
> gained only by purity of heart and through the illumination of
> the Holy Spirit.[3]

Note the elements involved. The goal is to enter into the marrow, to read deeply, to reach the underground veins of the
Word. He points out the road, first negatively, then positively.
Human science and erudition are said to be fundamentally inadequate, even if their subject is the Bible. No technique gives
access to a vital experience of the Word. The crucial factor is
the light of the Spirit, a free gift that comes from him, its
source. But the gift must be actively received. It presupposes
on our part an attitude of radical receptivity, namely, purity of
heart won through ascetical struggle. Thus the spiritual life

[1] See S. Marsili, *Giovanni Cassiano ed Evagrio Pontico*, Rome 1936.
[2] Bernard, *In Cant.*, serm. 62 (PL 183, 1079).
[3] Cassian, *Coll.* XIV, 9 (*Sourc. chrét.*, 54, 195). See also Bede, *In Marc.*, 8
(PL 82, 118).

coalesces in hearing; it influences it and determines its fruit. The Word is the saving power of God insofar as it is accepted. And it is accepted when the heart has opened its doors to the gift. Our gaze, says Cassian, must be pure. Every kind of impurity obscures its clarity, like a veil that prevents us from seeing. Those whose gaze of faith has been made penetrating by purity of heart are the only ones who understand. "For the one singing the psalms understands what is sung, the one traveling the road of innocence with a pure heart." There is no room for biblical intellectualism, much less the eloquence of oratory. The latter often serves only to hide our inner emptiness from the eyes of those who have not yet learned to recognize the true nature of spiritual knowledge. These are Cassian's words.

It is a pleasant surprise to find this theme repeated in the Instruction of the Biblical Commission on the teaching of Sacred Scripture. The exegete can discern the *sensus plenus* only to the extent that he or she possesses purity of heart.[4] As Gregory would say, it is not only a question of the "fullness of the Book" that can be attained by philological methods, but of the "fullness of the Word" that lies at the end of a spiritual journey and leads not to dead knowledge, but to a living understanding.[5]

Faith and humility

According to Cassian, one of the fruits of purity of heart is a penetrating gaze. But this is not the gaze of natural understanding; it is the gaze of faith. Or if you prefer, it is the gaze of understanding, enlightened by faith and endowed with the gifts of the Holy Spirit, especially wisdom and understanding. Such a gaze attains vital knowledge.[6]

Vital indeed, for it is a gaze that is able to recognize Christ in Scripture. Whoever knows him, enters into life.[7] And since

---

[4] *Acta Apost. Sedis*, 42/17 (1950) 501; *Ench. Bibl.*, 2nd ed., 599.
[5] Gregory, *In Reg.*, IV, 4, 49 (PL 79, 267–68).
[6] See Origen, *In Ex.* hom. 4, n. 5 (PG 12, 320–21).
[7] Paschasius, *In Lam.* lib. II (PL 120, 1105a).

we are in the supernatural realm, it will not be enough to re-
fine our research methods. We cannot reap the fruits of the
sacred page by pure human investigation, as if this were one
of the liberal arts or one of the sciences. Above all, we will
need to pray.[8] "The most important thing is to pray for understanding," said Augustine.[9] Such knowledge of Scripture is
essentially a contemplative activity. A medieval described it
this way: "To seek ourselves in God and God in ourselves."[10]
As the prologue to *Dei Verbum* says, following Augustine,
hearing involves the exercise of all the theological virtues:
"For [this holy synod] wants the whole world to hear the sum-
mons to salvation, so that through hearing it may believe,
through belief it may hope, through hope it may come to love."

Here is rooted the need for another spiritual attitude. Alcuin
calls it "devout humility,"[11] and Cassian "humility of heart."[12]
The Word of God is too great, and we are too small to approach it with presumption or intellectual pride. Our forehead
must be prostrate in the dust. This writer will not easily forget
that this was precisely the attitude adopted by Professor Zolli
(the former rabbi of Rome, converted to Catholicism by Pius
XII). It was his graphic expression of our nothingness before
the Word. On that occasion, I saw him embody that biblical
sense of the Word which has become so weak with us.

Augustine's experience on this subject is both typical and
eloquent:

> Accordingly I turned my attention to the holy scriptures to find
> out what they were like. What I see in them today is something
> not accessible to the scrutiny of the proud nor exposed to the

---

[8] Idem, *De fide*, c. 1: "First you must seek . . ., but no, I am not saying
you must *seek* faith; you must pray for it" (1389cd).

[9] Augustine, *Doctr. Christ.* III, 37, 56 (PL 34, 89). Many texts from
Jerome that insist on the need for prayer in order to understand Scripture
are cited by D. Gorge, op.cit., 190, nn. 1 and 2.

[10] Peter de Celle, *De afflictione et lectione,* in J. Leclercq, *La spiritualité de
Pierre de Celle,* op.cit., 238.

[11] Alcuin, *Epist.* I (PL 100, 139a).

[12] Cassian, *Coll.,* XIV, 10 (*Sourc. chrét.,* 54, 195).

gaze of the immature, something lowly as one enters but lofty as one advances further, something veiled in mystery. At that time, though, I was in no state to enter, nor prepared to bow my head and accommodate myself to its ways. My approach then was quite different from the one I am suggesting now: when I studied the Bible and compared it with Cicero's dignified prose, it seemed to me unworthy. My swollen pride recoiled from its style and my intelligence failed to penetrate to its inner meaning. Scripture is a reality that grows along with little children, but I disdained to be a little child and in my high and mighty arrogance regarded myself as grown up.[13]

Elsewhere Augustine summarizes the same experience in one sentence: "Proud as I was, I dared to seek that which only the humble can find."[14] Looking back, he realizes that then he was closing the door to God.

Hence our attitude before the Word must be marked by profound humility. This has serious consequences. First, we will approach it with that sense of the sacred which is inevitable whenever we approach the divine: with fear and trembling. The process of desacralization taking place in the Church today, legitimate in many ways, cannot and must not dissolve the aura of mystery in which God has wrapped his Word. It is right to eliminate from church institutions that which is excessively "sacred" and human in origin, but not the authentic "sacred" placed there by God. God humbled his eternal Word in our poor human language, with humans as instruments. Even before that, he placed his message in the living experience of a community and willed that it be transmitted to us in the existential form it assumed in this human context.

Think of the role of the early community in the transmission of the Gospel. The sacred writer who composed the final text was not a machine taking dictation. The message was filtered through his genius, his psyche, his theological and pastoral concerns. We are grateful to modern exegesis for having explained all this. But it is only so that we might kneel in adoration before this wonderful condescension, no less wonderful

---

[13] Augustine, *Confess.*, lib. III, c. 5, n. 9.
[14] Idem, *Serm.* 63 (PL 38, 424).

than that of the incarnation. In the presence of Jesus of Nazareth who chose to share our human condition, let us not forget the greatness of the living God whose sacrament he is. Likewise, in the presence of the poor human words in which he humbled his Wisdom, let us not forget the transcendence and holiness of the divine Word which became incarnate therein so that we might understand it. As we admire the condescension of a God who humbles himself precisely because he is the Most High, we feel our hearts swell with gratitude and humility.[15]

This does not prevent investigation and research on our part. If human language is the means, we will certainly need to analyze it with the help of philology. But our internal attitude is not that of philologist analyzing Homer or Livy. The content of this language is a divine Word which is mystery. We are moved, not by curiosity[16] but admiration. Our humble question arises from the awe we feel at the wonder of God's works, prompting us to search the great mystery in a spirit of reverent prayer.[17] "With hearts bowed, with obedient hearts,"

---

[15] "Hence, in sacred scripture, without prejudice to God's truth and holiness, the marvelous 'condescension' of eternal wisdom is plain to be seen, 'that we may come to know the ineffable loving-kindness of God and see for ourselves the thought and care he has given to accommodating his language to our nature.' Indeed the words of God, expressed in human language, are in every way like human speech, just as the Word of the eternal Father, when he took on himself the weak flesh of human beings, became like them." The text cited is from John Chrysostom, *In Gen.* 3, 8, hom. 17, 1 (PG 53, 134).

[16] The title of an anonymous twelfth-century work is typical: *De praescientia Dei contra curiosos.* See M.D. Chenu, *Culture et théologie à Jumièges après l'ère féodale,* in the volume *Jumièges. Congrès scientifique du XIIIᵉ centenaire,* Rouen 1955, 780. Rupert entitled one chapter of his work *De voluntate Dei* thus: "Scrupuli quidam curiosorum, qui Deum malum velle argutantur" (PL 170, 440). Bernard writes: "Understanding, if it tries to break the seal of faith, is reckoned an intruder, a searcher of majesty" *De cons.* V, 6 (PL 182, 790). Those who studied the sacred text with an intellectual curiosity that was judged intemperate were branded with the quasi-technical term "searchers of the (divine) majesty."

[17] See the text cited by H. de Lubac, op.cit., I, 103.

we ask the heavenly Teacher for a ray of light. That is all we can receive here below: "A little bead of light."[18] The ancients do invite us to seek, but to seek in moderation.[19] The sense of mystery precludes the naïve claim that we can capture it within our narrow and limited concepts. Our little human arguments bear no relation to the truth revealed to us by God in Scripture.[20] "He who has set limits to all things cannot be imprisoned within the limits of dialectics," exclaimed a Cistercian in the face of the first attempts at "rational" exegesis.[21]

If Truth is not reducible to the laws of our mind, then the latter must cease to impose its categories and mental structures on the Word. What is needed is just the opposite: it must get rid of these categories and humbly adopt those of the Word. He is Light and we are darkness. Humility finally becomes that total openness by which the soul obediently lets itself be formed by the thought of God.

Recollection

Finally, religious listening requires an atmosphere of silence and inner calm. We need to create in the day's rhythm a contemplative pause where the hubbub of business does not intrude to disturb us. John XXIII, in a talk to the Trappists, recalled a wonderful text from Bernard, part of which reads as follows: "There we are occupied with God . . . and give ourselves to holy reading. Constant is the silence, and the absence of all worldly cares compels us to meditate on the things of heaven."[22] In the place where we do our personal Scripture reading, we must create, as it were, a little monastic alcove—if not in our external surroundings, at least in the sanctuary of

---

[18] Rupert, *De Trin., In Ex.* I, 37 (PL 167, 604b); see *De divinis officiis*, III, 14 (CCL, *Cont. Med.* 7, 85).

[19] Idem, *De Trin., In Gen.* II, 20 (PL 167, 265bc). Ibid. *In Ex.* I, 2 (568a) etc.

[20] Bernard, *Epist.* 189, 4 (PL 182, 355c).

[21] Nicolaus of Clairvaux, *In Nativ.* serm. II, 7 (PL 184, 837d). See J. Leclercq, *L'amour des lettres*, op.cit., 190ff, where many similar texts are cited.

[22] Bernard, *Epist.* 78, 4 (PL 182, 193).

our heart. Then a mysterious and intimate communication is created between reader and Word. Peacefully striving to be recollected, I focus completely on listening. I put all my energy into it: not only my head, but also my heart in the gospel sense of the innermost center of my being. I am wholly present before the One who speaks to me. A Protestant exegete has expressed this concisely: "Adhere totally to the text, and refer what it says to yourself."[23] Earlier, Ambrose spoke of the soul that "devotes itself completely to the Word."[24] We know that "the Word" is not just a word (a text, as Bengel used to say); it is a Person. Our full attention must express itself in total adherence, full submission. We unconditionally surrender to the God who speaks. In the presence of the great Object, the soul lets itself be absorbed in what it is contemplating. It adheres to it in love and gives itself without reserve. But now we have gone beyond the subject of this section which deals with the moral dispositions. We have crossed over into the very heart of reading, which will be explained later.

In summary, we can say that tradition links understanding of Scripture to perfection of life. Our progress in transcending the poor things of this world[25] to adhere to the living God is measured and determined by our knowledge of the Word. If this is to be true, it must call upon all our spiritual powers. Only "those who are perfect" can reach the full light.[26]

Diligence

The prophet Amos, paradoxically, presents the fullness of time as a period of famine: "The time is surely coming, says the Lord God, when I will send a famine on the land; not a famine of bread, or a thirst for water, but of hearing the word of the Lord" (Amos 8:11). One who is spiritual is one who is

---

[23] Cited by L. Bouyer, *Introduzione alla vita spirituale*, Italian tr., Turin 1965, 72.

[24] Ambrose, *In Ps.* 118, VI, 8 (PL 15, 1270).

[25] Bede, *In Marc.* 8 (PL 92, 218b).

[26] Jerome, *In Is.* (PL 24, 266b).

hungry and thirsty. Only the Word can satisfy this craving. That is why Scripture is often presented as bread or as a fountain of living water.[27] Gregory would call it "a banquet of delights which is a prelude to that of heaven."[28] In the natural order, hunger and thirst are not under our control; they are stimuli that arise from a physical need. It is the same in the spiritual order. Hunger for the Word is a need of love. The drought that creates this thirst is the fire of love;[29] it is the "soul obsessed with Scripture" which Jerome admired in Origen.[30] Lack of reading is an unbearable fast which saps the life of the spirit.[31] Love inevitably brings with it an irresistible need to know. Everything pertaining to the beloved takes on special interest and becomes the object of intense searching. Augustine's love of Truth, which prompted his search and made it so fruitful, is of this kind. It is not intellectualism. It is the discovery of the mystery of a Person deeply loved, in whom every truth comes together like the lines on his face. He *is* the Truth, and every text of Scripture speaks of him.

[27] See Jerome, *Epist.*, 30, 13. He points out to Paula that whoever reads the holy books and strives to penetrate their teaching breaks this heavenly bread (PL 22, 244). Gregory, *In Ezech.* I, 10, 5, clarifies the image further. The Word is both food and drink. It is drink in the historical sense of being directly accessible with no need to be chewed; it is food in the mystical sense that it is discovered only when its wrapping is broken open through an adequate explanation. This nourishment, like that of the body, must be daily (PL 76, 887).

[28] Gregory, *Moral.* 16, 24: "To abound with delights because of the Almighty means to be filled with his love at the banquet of Sacred Scripture. The joys we find there are in proportion to the various interpretations that present themselves for our spiritual progress. Sometimes the literal sense is enough to nourish us, sometimes the allegorical morality concealed in the text re-creates us inwardly, another time we are held suspended in contemplation, which blazes with the light of eternity in the darkness of this present life" (PL 75, 1132).

[29] We are referring to the text of Ferreoli cited above in chapter 1, note 2.

[30] Jerome, *Epist.*, 84, 8 (PL 22, 750).

[31] Ferreoli, *Regula*, 28 (Ed. Holste-Brockie, *Codex Regularum* I, Graz 1957, 164).

> O eternal Word, word of my God, I want to spend my life listen-
> ing to you . . . in order to learn everything from you . . . I want
> to gaze upon you always and remain under your great light.

These words are from the famous "elevation" written by Sister
Elizabeth of the Trinity on the eve of her profession, November 21, 1904. This is not merely a mystic's impromptu outburst
in a moment of grace; it is a constant of every true search for
God. The council said: "[Let them] immerse themselves in the
scriptures by constant spiritual reading and diligent study."[32]
This is vital contact of communion, adherence in faith and love.
It is an identification that by its nature speaks of continuity. We
arrive at it through diligent reading which is characterized by
total commitment. This inner listening is the prerequisite for
effective external proclamation. It gives access to the super-
abundant riches of the divine Word. But what will stimulate
us to such diligent and total commitment except hunger born
of love?

Tradition presents us with striking examples. Jerome, the
doctor lectionis, sums up his experience in a famous exhortation:
"Let sleep steal upon you with a book in your hand, and let
the sacred page catch your drooping head."[33] He falls asleep,
disappointed that he cannot read longer. The practice of reading becomes such a second nature that not even sleep can interrupt it; his lips instinctively continue to move as they do when
he is reading.[34] The early monks drank from this source with
an unquenchable thirst. They would softly whisper the sacred
words with their lips in order to imprint them not only on
their mind but also on their body. "His mouth was constantly
ruminating the sacred words," says Peter the Venerable of one
of his monks.[35] John of Gorze's biographer uses a picturesque

[32] DV 25.

[33] Jerome, *Epist.* 22, 17 *Ad Eustochium* (PL 22, 404).

[34] To cite one example, here is what Tritemius says of Rupert of Deutz:
"From the time he entered the monastery as a youth, he was kept awake
by Sacred Scripture. It seemed he could not stop meditating on it, even
during sleep. His tongue and lips kept moving as if he were reading"
(Ruperti Tuitiensis, *Opera omnia,* I, Cologne 1667 [3]).

[35] Peter the Venerable, *De mirac.,* I, 20 (PL 189, 887).

image: "Like a bee, he rummaged through the psalms inces-
santly, whispering to himself."[36] Are these a hagiographer's
pious exaggerations? Perhaps, to some extent. But there is too
much evidence in every genre of writing—from rules and treatises to letters—for it is not to be based on a marvelous reality
whose secret we have lost. The Word is present in every activity of the day. It is a lamp that illumines every action by cast-
ing God's light over it.

The work of patiently copying codices naturally allows the
soul to become "saturated with reading."[37] Reading even accompanied meals, "so that not only the body is fed, but the
starving soul is nourished by the Word of God."[38] Do you
spend time with your brothers in familiar conversation? Speak
about the spiritual joys of bible reading.[39] Is your heart over-
whelmed with anguish? Reading a single sacred page will be
enough to dispel it.[40] Are you about to die? The words of the
Psalms transform even the pain of agony into a sacrifice of
praise.[41] Sulpicius Severus wrote of St. Martin: "Not an hour or
moment ever passed that he did not devote himself to prayer
or attend to reading."[42] A literal paradox, these words express
an ideal that later monks could not forget. Reading fills their
life. It marks the days and nights, it alternates with work in a
harmonious rhythm,[43] it accompanies the vigil and precedes

---

[36] John of St. Arnulf, *Life of John of Gorze*, n. 80 (PL 137, 280).

[37] Jerome, *Epist.* 125, 11: ". . . copy out manuscripts, so that your hand
may earn you food and your soul be saturated with reading" (PL 22,
1079).

[38] *Regula Tarnatensis,* 8 (Ed. Holste-Brockie, cit. I, 184). Models for this
typical monastic custom can already be found in the great Fathers, for example, Origen: see Jerome, *Epist.* 43, 1 (see note 44 below).

[39] See F.M. Powicke, *Walter Daniel's Life of Ailred of Rievaulx*, London
1950, 40.

[40] Aelred, *De oner.* (PL 195, 476bc).

[41] See Jerome, *Epist.* 108, 28: "She was at the point of death, yet she kept
repeating the same verses, . . . she was changing the death-rattle that
ends human life into praise of the Lord" (PL 22, 904). What is being described here is the death of Paula.

[42] Sulpicius Severus, *Vita beati Martini,* 26 (PL 20, 175–76).

[43] Ferreoli, *Regula,* 28 (Ed. Holste-Brockie, op.cit., 164).

sleep,[44] it fills life and sanctifies death. It is like the connective tissue of life, earthly psalmody being a preparation for the inexpressible conversation of heaven. Life becomes an anticipation of paradise: "Paradise is your home,"[45] or as a modern writer says, "the foretaste of eternal happiness."[46]

Was all this the exclusive appanage of virgins or monks? No, it was an ideal for everyone, even if it was lived with special fervor by religious. The following invitation, from a famous letter of Gregory, was addressed to the emperor's physician, a layman:

> Seek, then, to meditate every day on the words of your Creator. Learn to know the heart of God in the words of God, so that you may desire eternal goods more ardently and your soul may be enkindled with greater longing for the goods of heaven.[47]

From diligence to familiarity [48]

Obviously, diligent and constant reading creates familiarity with the world of the Bible. But this does not come from a first reading. If a quick voyage of discovery is all we want, we will be disappointed. The beauty of this fascinating world will be hidden from us; upon entering it, we will feel as though everything is foreign. We cannot venture into the Bible as tourists; we must become inhabitants of the land. We need to retrace our steps, stop and reflect at each site in order to explore it in depth. To become part of this world we must enter it, immerse ourselves in it in order to be absorbed by it. Then it will reveal

[44] Jerome says of Ambrose (*Epist.* 43, 1): "Day and night it was [his] habit to make reading follow upon prayer, and prayer upon reading without a break" (PL 22, 478). Jerome says of Paula that often the morning sun found her absorbed in reading and prayer (*Epist.* 45, 3): "All night long she would beg the Lord for mercy, and often the sun found her still praying. The psalms were her music, the Gospels her conversation. . . ." (PL 22, 481).

[45] Jerome, *Epist.* 22, 19 (PL 22, 406). We know the place occupied by the theme of the "return to paradise" in ancient monastic literature.

[46] R. Garrigou-Lagrange, *De sanctificatione sacerdotum*, Rome 1946, 24.

[47] Gregory, *Epist.* 31, 54 (PL 77, 706).

[48] The expression is inspired by Jerome, *Epist.* 45, 2 (PL 22, 481).

to us the charm of its secret places. The same thing happens with certain pieces of classical music. Only after repeated listening do we detect the secret harmonies, discover the language, catch the dominant themes.

At that point familiarity produces perfect harmony. The Word of God molds the secret depths of our soul, becomes part of our inner world, seeps into our mind as if by osmosis. Cassian's discussion of this in *Conference XIV* is unsurpassed. He sets up clear conditions for reaching the objective. We must lay aside all earthly cares and thoughts and apply ourselves to *lectio* diligently—or better, constantly. Our ears are always open, eager for the saving words; our lips are always ready to utter them. This is not a momentary contact, like our perception of some vague odor in the air. It is a lasting communion with the Word, as constant as our breathing. What happens then? The reading becomes part of your inner world. The words are strong and richly evocative. A few pages earlier, he said that a time would come when continuous meditation would impregnate your soul and mold it in his image.[49]

Tradition offers us outstanding examples of such assimilation. Think of St. Bernard. His every word is Scripture. His language is a patchwork of bible texts stitched together by the spontaneous and often clever game of mental associations. This is a typical phenomenon that Leclercq calls "reminiscence." One text automatically recalls another, and a cascade of citations follows. But there is a breath of undeniable newness in those pages. It is not mechanical repetition. Hugh Metel calls it a new language:[50] the ancient words are filtered through his mind and pass through the crucible of his fervent heart. They become "the Bible of his heart."[51] And when they pour forth in speech or writing, in addition to the ever-present divine message, they present us with a piece of Bernard's soul.

[49] Cassian, *Coll.* XIV, nn. 10 and 15 (ed.cit., 195, 200).

[50] Hugh of Mettelus, *Epist. ad S. Bern:* "Your manner of expressing yourself is new. You speak a new language when you speak with power of the divine mysteries" (PL 182, 687–88).

[51] Thus the biographer of Aelred of Rievaulx; see F.M. Powicke, op.cit., 41. Since Aelred was a disciple of Bernard, this is *a fortiori* true of his

Bernard's is not an isolated case. It is simply the most appealing expression of a phenomenon more or less universal at the time. Why could something similar not be done today? It is a task for spiritual men and women of every age. They need to filter the eternal message of the Bible through the religious sensibility of their time and give it an up-to-date flavor that will attract their contemporaries. It is an urgent task, one that complements the work of catechesis. For the latter, it could be a lifegiving breath that comes from lived experience.

But anyone who wishes to do this will need to follow the council's exhortation: "Let them always have the Scriptures in their hands." Only then will there be a mysterious and intimate communion between the soul and the Word, a constant sharing of secrets. It is not, says Gregory, the kind of fleeting or occasional meeting that reveals to me the features of a person's face. It is a diligent and prolonged conversation that leads me into the innermost recesses: "If we unite ourselves to it [Scripture] diligently, we enter into its mind as if in familiar conversation."[52] There is created "a bond between our mind and the mind of Scripture,"[53] indeed, perfect harmony. Again, as Gregory would say, the Word becomes an experience from which darts a red-hot spark as from cold flint.[54] A blazing fire is enkindled in the soul, one that is capable of spreading. This is the outcome. But first we must knock, patiently and insistently, at the door of those blessed words—knock and be ready, with a desire to understand. Sparks are not always produced at first striking.

Wisdom

The Bible's overall content is the mystery of salvation. The Word is an instrument that serves this mystery. "It is the

---

master. We know that in its semantic evolution the word "library" came to refer to the Bible.

[52] Gregory, *Moral.*, IV, 1 (PL 75, 633).

[53] This was said of Bernard; see Dumontier, *Saint Bernard et la Bible,* op.cit., 161.

[54] Gregory, *In Ezech.*, II, 10, 1 (PL 76, 1058).

power of God for salvation to everyone who has faith," says Paul (Rom 1:16). It is not just a source of knowledge or information. God did not speak simply to feed our mind or tickle our imagination. If that were the case, I would read only for understanding. But if I take in my hands a living Word that is power for salvation,[55] then I read in order to live and be saved. And although it is truly a science since it allows us to glimpse the mystery of God,[56] it is a "science of salvation."[57]

The cognitive aspect is obviously not excluded. But the term is understood in its full biblical meaning: vital knowledge that corresponds to God's knowledge of us. When God "knows" a being, he cares about it, loves it, chooses it, showers it with gifts, and binds it as if it shared the same destiny. "You only have I known of all the families of the earth" says God to Israel through the lips of Amos (Amos 3:2). The covenant, too, is a form of knowledge. The same nuptial imagery applied with such insistence by the Bible to the Lord and his people (Hosea, Ezekiel, Canticle, Psalm 45) illustrates this theme. A medieval monk sums up the elements in a few short lines:

> The term "knowledge," in the language of Scripture, refers to a relationship of the soul realized in an ineffable experience. To what do the nuptial metaphors or the Pauline expression "Then I shall know even as I am known" refer, if not to that eternal exchange of love, to that torrent of happiness with which God will flood the loving soul?[58]

Our knowledge of God is a response to his knowledge of us. That is its origin and model. The Word is its means and instrument. Through *lectio divina* I know God. But it is a knowledge that translates into assent, surrender, a commitment that involves my whole life. All this is summed up in Paul's "obedient faith" of which the council says that it leads one "to

---

[55] See the section above: "The saving power of God."

[56] See the section above: "A kiss of eternity."

[57] William Firmat, *Exhortatio*, ed. J. Leclercq, *Anal. monast.* II, 32.

[58] Rupert, *De glorif. Trin.*, VII, 16 (PL 169, 158d–159ab). See ibid. II, 11 (41c, 42b). Bernard, *In Cant.* 82 (PL 183, 1181). William of St. Thierry, *In Cant.* I (PL 180, 505–7).

freely commit oneself entirely to God, making the full submission of intellect and will to him."[59] The cognitive aspect is closely connected to the volitional and existential aspects. The whole human person is involved in this knowlege. That is why the ancients preferred the term "wisdom."

Study and lectio divina

By insisting on the sapiential aspect, we do not mean to exclude the appropriate role of study, and normally, the need for it. All we are saying is that its role with regard to *lectio divina* is introductory. It prepares us for the vital assimilation that can take place only in prayer. We want to insist on a conviction that is deeply rooted in all Christian tradition: knowledge that does not lead to love is vain. The Truth must be a principle of life. No one disagrees in theory, but we often deny it in practice. We all know the real risk of Bible study that becomes nothing but philology at the scientific level, and a pedantic exercise in the cold accumulation of facts at the textbook level. The very soul of Scripture perishes in such research. Surely that is not why God has spoken.

But serious study, a genuine tool of spiritual research, can be of greatest service to *lectio divina*. Jerome insisted on this by his words and the example of his life, in which learning and contemplation were so harmoniously allied. Criticism is at the service of fervent piety.[60] Meditation, that most faithful companion, is always found alongside knowledge of Hebrew.[61] In that Roman milieu, so pretentious and casual in its interpretation of the sacred Books, his rallying cry was *let us work hard*. His friends became friends of science; there sprang up in his

---

[59] DV 5.

[60] See *In Is.* (PL 24, 477): to understand Scripture we must make use of "the ear of the heart."

[61] Jerome, *Epist.* 50, 1: "Has the learning I gained from the Jews been for nothing? And what of systematic daily meditation on the law, the prophets and the apostles, which I have done since my youth until the present?" (PL 22, 513).

school a new kind of intellectual asceticism. Men and women were not satisfied with the "muddy streams" of rough translations but came to the pure springs of the *veritas hebraica*.

What, then, of modern exegesis and its much better tools? Since it give us a more exact knowledge of literary forms, it lets us see beyond the poetry to the Word of God. We see the authentic nature of a saving event beneath the fanciful garb in which it is clothed. Correct historical perspective lets us situate each bit of information in its place as a stage in revelation and a moment in God's great plan. It makes us fall to our knees in adoration or to reverently exclaim: "How wonderful are your works!"

Biblical theology isolates themes and traces their development in the course of salvation history. These themes give us a vivid sense of the unity of the two Testaments, which fills us with joy. Conducted in this way, study is already very close to the spiritual life. But it is not yet *lectio sacra*. It prepares for it and makes it more valuable because of the spiritual "culture" it provides. But it does not yet lead to prayer. All Bible study must produce this fruit as the ultimate goal of all research.

But when the purposes of study are avowedly scientific, the distinction is even clearer. To be sure, science is legitimate and even necessary; but it exists on another plane and breathes a different air. An encounter with it can help us describe better the characteristics of *lectio*. The monks often did this when faced with the new scholasticism. The latter marks the great watershed in the evolution of Christian thought between the "wisdom" of the Fathers and the "science" of modern theology.[62] Study is concerned with scientific certitude; *lectio* wishes to nourish a spiritual experience. Study takes place on the objective and detached level of investigation; *lectio* takes place in the contemplative atmosphere of prayer. Professional exegetes strive to prescind from personal feelings. Spiritual persons approach the Bible like Bernard, with open mouth and heart. Fervent before they start to read, they read in order to become even more fervent. Their aim is not to construct a science, but

---

[62] See J. Leclercq, *L'amour des lettres*, op.cit., especially 179–216; M. Magrassi, *Teologia e storia nel pensiero di Ruperto*, op.cit., 36–46.

wisdom, which is contemplative knowledge. They do not proceed by way of a specific analytic technique, but trust the intutions of their grace-filled soul.

This does not mean that *lectio* is reduced to pious reading, with no serious effort at study. Rupert of Deutz, that great practitioner of *lectio*, speaks of a hand-to-hand struggle with the Book, similar to that of Jacob with the angel: "Sweet struggle, happier than any peace."[63] But this combat takes place in a different setting; it is associated with the ardor of contemplation, the ardor of holy study.[64]

Some of the texts that reflect a genuine experience can reconstruct this setting better than all our subtle distinctions. There is the case of a famous Paris master, Abelard's equal in dialectic disputes. Inspired by a bolt from the blue, he gave up his studies and the world to join the Abbey of Anchin. As always, life in the cloister involved extended contact with the Bible. But Goswin, an unrepentant intellectual, approached it as a philologist. Consequently, *lectio* left him dry and flat. Instead of creating hunger, it provoked disgust. A second conversion was needed to complete the first. Gregory the Great was the instrument. With his help, Goswin came to realize that wasting time with the sacred text building intellectual castles is not what matters. We must approach it with deep reverence and devotion in order to build within ourselves the kingdom of Christ and nourish prayer. If that text does not reverberate in our life, it remains a dead letter. And so he returned to the Bible renewed:

> He took Gregory's advice as if it were addressed to him: "Have you sinned, and now that you regret your unlawful deeds, you wish to learn how to repent? There you will find laments. Do you wish to console your mind with the hope of heavenly joys? There you will find a song for your comfort."[65] He read those words. He read them and admired them, and in his admiration he reread them several times. And while his eyes were applied to the text, his soul was devoted to its meaning. Through the

[63] Rupert, *In Cant.*, praef. (PL 168, 837–38).
[64] Idem, *De vict. Verbi Dei*, praef. (PL 169, 1217–18).
[65] Gregory, *In Ezech.* I, 9, 34 (PL 76, 886a).

Scriptures the fervor of the Holy Spirit was setting his soul afire. . . . Boredom was replaced by mirth . . . and courage shone in his actions.[66]

Gregory explained this in his famous *Homily III on Ezekiel.*[67] What is the meaning of the face and the flight of the four living creatures who appear in Ezekiel's first vision? "The face signifies knowledge and the wings the face of contemplation." Two kinds of knowledge correspond to two ways of reading. On the one hand, there is clear and precise knowledge, the object of teaching, the rule of faith, the deposit to be faithfully handed on. It corresponds to a kind of reading we might call exegetical or theological. On the other hand, there is the flight, "not an intellectual representation but a spiritual movement that raises the mind to contemplation."[68] Gregory loves to say that they fly with the wings of contemplation. They hover in a higher region that transcends the area of scientific knowledge. While he appreciates and uses scientifica data, that is not the object of his concern. What interests him is the fruit of a reading that may be called contemplative.

Here Gregory speaks for a whole tradition. Behind him lies the impressive experience of generations who, before or after him, pored tirelessly over the sacred Book in this spirit. Fixing their contemplative gaze on it ("the soul's attentive gaze" a follower of Augustine calls it[69]), they drew from that source nourishment for a deep spiritual life. Mystical contemplation is the end of a journey that begins with the sacred Book. It passes through the teaching of faith, leads to formation, creates moral attitudes modeled on the Word, and culminates in that "sweetest experience of divine love, which with its ineffable sweetness unites us to the supreme God."[70] A true journey of union, it raises the human heart to the heart of God.

[66] The passage is found in the *Vita Goswini* (ms. 821 of the Library of Douai, fol. 166) and is cited more fully by J. Leclercq, *La Liturgia e i paradossi cristiani,* Italian version, Milan 1967, 180–281.

[67] See PL 76, 805ff.

[68] H. de Lubac, op.cit., I, 639.

[69] Thus Hervé of Bourg-Dieu (PL 181, 19b).

[70] Anselm of Canterbury, *De S. Anselmi similitudinibus,* c. 194 (PL 159, 708).

Returning to the main point of our analysis, we can say that study is the fruit of human research techniques. It leads to scientific knowledge. *Lectio* is a gift of grace, received in an atmosphere of prayer. It leads to an experience. The two are not opposed; on the contrary, they must be integrated. But the first is directed to the second as to its goal. Only then does the Word bear fruit:

> Blessed are they who know, with the happy tasting that comes from experience, how sweetly and wonderfully the Lord is pleased to give understanding of the Scriptures in prayer and meditation.[71]

The taste of a happy experience

It is God himself who is revealed in a happy experience. God's influence takes the form of two gifts of the Holy Spirit: understanding and wisdom. The first perfects faith by way of a certain penetrating vision.[72] We read "within" the word and our understanding of its mystery is deepened. This understanding is not directly related either to intelligence or degree of scientific preparation. It is a gift of God, given by preference to the pure and simple of heart: "Simplicity comprehends God and understands him" notes the *Imitation of Christ*.

The gift of wisdom, on the other hand, perfects charity by way of a certain experiential tasting.[73] It leads us to savor the divine Word, because it creates a kind of connaturality between the soul and Scripture. We read it under the guidance of the same Spirit who inspired it. This results in a joyful experience, which the classics of *lectio* love to describe. Here is a page from William of St. Thierry:

> Wisdom is rightly placed in the mind. . . . For the mind is a particular strength of the soul whereby we cleave to God and enjoy God. This enjoyment, however, is a sort of divine savor, so wisdom comes from savor. This savor is a sort of tasting.

---

[71] Anonymous, *Sermon on Emmaus*, n. 20 (PL 184, 976c).
[72] St. Thomas, *Sent.* III, d. 34, 2.
[73] Ibid.

And no one is worthy to articulate this tasting unless he has deserved to taste, for [Scripture] says: *Taste and see that the Lord is sweet.*

This is the taste which the Spirit of understanding gives us in Christ, namely, the understanding of Scripture and of the sacraments of God. So it is that when the Lord appeared to his disciples after the resurrection, when, as the evangelist says, *he opened to them the meaning that they might understand the Scriptures.* For when we begin not only to understand but even somehow, I say, to touch and handle the inner meaning of Scriptures and the virtue of God's mysteries and sacraments with the hand of experience—which does not happen except by some special sense of conscience and by the discipline of an experience which understands, yes, and I go on to say, which reads inwardly within itself and senses the goodness and the virtue of God which the work of grace itself accomplishes by its powerful goodness and effective virtue within the sons of grace—then at last wisdom accomplishes what is proper to it. Then it judges those who are worthy; by its anointing, it teaches all things. Then, by having affixed the seal of God's goodness to us, it imprints and conforms [to itself] by this anointing everything calmed and gentled within us. . . .

O blessed knowledge wherein is contained eternal life! That life comes from this tasting, because to taste is to understand.[74]

The teaching contained in these lines can be summarized thus: at the most acute point of the soul is an active ability that unites us to God and enables us to taste God's presence. It cannot be expressed, but it could be called wisdom because it gives us a savory taste of divine things. It is a faculty that transcends the ordinary intellectual order. On the other hand, the analogy of taste and sweetness should not make us think of an easy movement of the senses. We are beyond the warmth of feeling as much as we are beyond cold intellectual pleasure. We are on a supernatural level. It is the Spirit of wisdom and understanding who creates in us this taste. God's activity, which cannot be precisely described, is both intuitive and

[74] William of St. Thierry, *De natura et dignitate amoris*, 10 (PL 184, 397c–99c) [Tr. Thomas X. Davis]. See Dumontier, *Saint Bernard et la Bible,* cit., especially 68–104.

experiential. It is intuitive because it presupposes direct contact with its object, albeit in the darkness of faith. This is indicated by the Scripture text: *Taste and see.* . . . It is experiential because we not only understand but touch with our hands the mystery within us, which has been incorporated into our spiritual life by becoming an experience. In this way we plumb the Scriptures, reaching the depths where lie the secrets of God. At the same time we plumb the depths of our soul, reading there the marvels wrought by grace. Thus the mystery of Scripture is seen in its close relationship to the spiritual life.

There are things, said St. Bernard, of which the intellect understands nothing unless accompanied by experience.[75] He is right; his observation is perennially valid. The Word of God is surely one of these things.

Dialogue

"Reading done by two people" is how Dumontier defines *lectio divina*. When sketching the meaning of the term, we already stressed the key idea that inspires it: the living presence of the Speaker who initiates the dialogue. When I read, he speaks to me; when I pray, I respond to him. This is the focal point of all spirituality of the Word. Everything we have said is invalid if it is not based on this profound faith insight. It is worth taking a moment to examine it more closely.

"The Word of the Lord came to me."

First, we need to grasp the importance of the fact that God speaks to us. This is the main feature of revealed religion. God is not content to let us search. The whole Bible stresses the primacy of the divine initiative. Augustine says that we would not have sought God if God had not first sought us.[76] It was

---

[75] Bernard, *In Cant.*, serm. 22, n. 2 (PL 183, 878c).

[76] A Persian poet, Eddin Attar, expresses his religious experience in similar terms: "For thirty years I went about seeking God. When, at the end of that time, I opened my eyes . . . I realized it was he who was seeking me."

not Israel who chose God, but God who chose Israel. Speaking of love, John observes that it was God who first loved us. The same must be said of that primordial reality, the Word. God is not only someone who listens to me. Before that, he is somone who *speaks* to me. The Word is the act by which he takes the initiative: he seeks me, enters my life, takes hold of it and molds it through the power of his love. It is, in a way, the central point of God's intervention in human life. Our history becomes sacred the moment he intervenes in it.

From this flows the basic Judeo-Christian attitude: listening. The Bible presents us with a people who listen: "Hear, O Israel." The Gospel message—as its heralds frequently stress—first requires hearers. It is the first act of Christian asceticism. The Rule for western monks begins with the words, "Listen, O son." The mystery religions tended toward seeing, but Judaism is the religion of hearing and obeying.

From the initial fact that God speaks to us flows the personal nature of religious relationships. Only in the word, in dialogue, does someone become for us a person.[77] The relationship is created by the word. Until I speak to God and God speaks to me, even though I might know everything about God, God is not a person for me. Once God speaks to me, God becomes a "thou" whom I address. At that precise moment authentic personal relationship begins. Religion is not exempt from this law. God is for me someone (in the full sense of the term) precisely because God addresses God's Word to me and I am able to respond. In this marvelous dialogue, the divine "I" addresses me as "thou." Only from this can an authentic religious relationship arise—one that is able to express itself in love and devotion.[78]

[77] This was the fundamental insight of the modern Jewish philosopher, Martin Buber. L. Bouyer, among others, has introduced us to him in various works of his; see, for example, *Introduzione alla vita spirituale*, cit., 21–22.

[78] Paul VI insisted on this in a talk given at his general Wednesday audience (see *L'Osservatore Romano*, 14 August 1969): "Never tire as you strive to elicit from the depths of your soul and with your inner voice this 'THOU!' addressed to the ineffable God, that mysterious Other who sees

Too often, God is seen only as an *object* of faith. All I have then is a set of truths to memorize, rather like dry grammar. I cannot enter into communion with the living God. No, he is first of all the *subject* of the relationship. God comes to meet me and addresses me through the free and sovereign initiative of God's love. Then for me, as for Abraham, God has a face and a voice. God calls me by name and speaks God's Word to me. And I fall on my knees before God like Thomas, with a cry of faith, "My Lord and my God."

The prophet's mission also arises from this initial experience: "The word of the Lord came to me." This technical expression marks the prophetic writings. It confronts us with that fundamental experience which gives meaning to the prophet's life and mission. It is a decisive experience, like a consuming inner fire, a disruptive force. Apparently it does not even allow attempts to resist. But it is so important that it makes the prophet's life "historical" and assigns him a task within the people of God. The *dabar Yahweh*, heard and transmitted, inserts the life of the prophet into the fabric of salvation history and determines its path. Everything else is nothing, doomed to sterility.

Apart from the special charism of inspiration, this prophetic experience is one that can be shared. Luke shows it at work in John the Baptist: "The word of God came to John son of Zechariah in the wilderness" (Luke 3:2). So aware is Luke of the historical importance of the event that he feels the need to situate it. He uses all the historical and geographical coordinates, bringing on stage emperors, tetrarchs, and high priests. The unusual solemnity of his preamble to chapter 3 is a surprise only to one who has not grasped the truly historical importance of the event: God is speaking one of his Words to a human being.

This is what happens in the life of each of us. Lest we had any doubts, the council reminded us that God, who spoke in the past in the Bible, continues to speak today with the

---

us, waits for us, loves us. Surely you will not be disappointed or abandoned but will feel the new joy of an exhilarating response: *Ecce adsum!* Here I am (Isa 58:9)."

Church, the spouse of God's Son, making the living voice of the Gospel ring out.[79] But the Church is not an abstraction. It is made up of people, and his mystery lives in the life of each one. Ambrose said that the Church is beautiful in its people. The Word addressed to all is at the same time addressed to each one:

> By this revelation, then, the invisible God, from the fullness of his love, addresses men and women as his friends, and lives among them, in order to invite and receive them into his own company.[80] In the sacred books the Father who is in heaven comes lovingly to meet his children, and talks with them.[81]

The privilege of Moses, with whom "the Lord spoke face to face, as one speaks to a friend" (Exod 33:13), inherited by the apostles (John 15:14-15), is transmitted to all the children of God.

The divine conversation

In this context, Leclercq's definition of *lectio* as "prayed reading" becomes fully clear. It is supported in some way by these words from *Dei Verbum:*

> [P]rayer should accompany the reading of sacred scripture, so that it becomes a dialogue between God and the human reader. For "we speak to him when we pray; we listen to him when we read the divine oracles."[82]

Reading and prayer are the two related phases of a single act, the two parts of the dialogue. Traditionally, prayer is considered a dialogue, but we do not always grasp the meaning of the term. A dialogue always presupposes two speakers, face to face. It presupposes that both express themselves and com-

---

[79] DV 8.
[80] Ibid. 2.
[81] Ibid. 21.
[82] DV 25, which cites Ambrose, *De off. ministr.* I, 20, 88 (PL 16, 50).

municate with each other through words. Otherwise there is only a monologue. Too often, prayer is reduced to this. If the two participants are far apart in rank and dignity, it is up to the higher to introduce and initiate the conversation. In this case, the two participants are the soul and God; the initiative must belong to God. What he says is what matters most. We could even say it is the *only* thing that matters.Thus prayer is first of all listening—listening to the one who speaks in Scripture. And *lectio*, when it is truly a listening to Someone, is already prayer. It is its first fundamental act. For this reason Christian prayer that does not begin with the Bible is inconceivable. The same holds true for Bible reading that does not ultimately lead to prayer.

This presupposes two things. We must know how to discern the presence of God in God's word, and the Word must be received as a personal message directly addressed to each of us. The first condition is one of the great faith insights illustrated at the beginning.[83] Here we need to stress that the living perception of this presence by faith is the basic condition for true dialogue. The Word must be discerned in the speaker's mouth, as Gregory the Great says.[84] Otherwise I could read a text but not hear the Word. Jerome says of St. Hilarion that "after the prayers and singing of the Psalms, he recited Scripture, which he knew by heart, as if he had seen God before him."[85] The ancients loved to say that Christ hides himself within the written letters. As they paged through a codex, they knew they were encountering him.[86] Even more: they could feel his heart beating in those words;[87] they were able to discover there his love. Gregory has an unforgettable formula: "Learn to know the heart of God in the words of God."[88] If he is present, then I

---

[83] In the section entitled *A living Book* (chapter III).

[84] Gregory, *Moral.*, XVI, 35, 43: "The souls of the just are present to the almighty Lord through their intention, and in his Scriptures they are, as it were, looking at his mouth" (PL 75, 1142d).

[85] Jerome, *Vita S. Hilarionis*, n. 10 (PL 23, 33).

[86] William Firmat, *Exhortatio* (ed. Leclercq, *Anal. monast.* II, 36).

[87] Godfrey of Admont, *Hom. dom.* 27 (PL 174, 339b).

[88] Gregory, *Epist.* 31, 54 (PL 77, 706).

truly receive a living Word. And if it comes from the heart of God, how can it not reach my heart? The dialogue has begun and is taking place in an atmosphere of love. One of the antiphons in the Roman Breviary says of St. Cecilia: "The glorious virgin kept the Gospel of Christ ever in her heart; day or night she never ceased praying and speaking with God" (Ant. Magn. II Vespers).

But the God who is present addresses that Word personally to me. Here again it is Gregory who speaks most eloquently: Scripture is a letter.[89] Unlike a book, a letter always bears a personal message. The historical view, which groups the different books of the Bible on a historical timeline, links them to a specific milieu and relates them to concrete historical facts. But unless it is accompanied by a theological view, it risks confining them to the field of archaeology. To be sure, the words have been fixed for millennia, "but he who causes us to hear them today, was already looking to us when he inspired them, and he is always there to speak to us, as if they were spoken at that moment for the first time."[90] So true is this that if God had not already said that Word, God would say it now for me.[91]

To sum up. When I pick up the sacred Book, the speaker is present before me as a divine "Thou." At that moment God speaks those words for me. God wishes to create a dialogue of love, to take hold of my life and insert it into God's life. What power there is in those words, if I receive them from God's lips in this way! They become truly able to reach the very depths of the human heart, "piercing until they divide soul from spirit." In the presence of a message so alive, relevant and personal, I pay full attention. The words of the young Samuel spring spontaneously to my lips: "Speak, Lord, for your servant is listening." My entire soul is present in that listening, which is then expressed in the adherence of faith and in total surrender.

[89] Ibid.: "A letter from almighty God to his creature."
[90] L. Bouyer, *Introduzione alla vita spirituale*, cit., 71.
[91] According to the already-cited formula of Gregory, *In Reg.* III, 5, 30 (PL 79, 216c).

A scene from the Gospel of Luke (10:39) offers us the most striking model of such listening: Mary, the sister of Lazarus, seated at the Lord's feet. She listens, that is to say, she eagerly drinks in the words from his lips. So deeply and joyfully intent is she on listening that she forgets everything else. For her at that moment, there is nothing else in the world worth worrying about. And the Lord gives her the reason: this is the one thing truly necessary.

Commitment

Diligent reading fed by hunger based on love—savory knowledge tasted in inner experience—dialogue with the living God that breaks into prayer upon receiving a living and personal Word: these are the elements of *lectio* as described thus far. They are major elements, already sufficient to describe it. But we are missing one, perhaps the most crucial. Prayer does not exhaust our response to God who speaks to us. Words are not enough, not even affections that touch our innermost heart. Concrete acts are needed. We respond with our whole life.

Listening is a very demanding activity. We can see this already on the psychological level. Other experiences such as seeing or touching involve considerable passivity and inertia. I establish contact with an objective reality placed before me. But listening is something else. I am placed before a person who wishes to establish communion with me, who intervenes in my life. By its nature this demands active participation. Attention is not enough; there must be a response that engages all our vital energies:

- God speaks. We listen and respond. That is prayer.

- God is revealed. We receive that ray of light shed on the mystery of God, and we commit our life to the gradual discovery of God's face. That is faith.

- God teaches. We model our mental world on that Truth. That is what Paul calls "doing the truth."

- When God speaks, God freely gives. In accepting the gift we enter into communion and say, "Make us an everlasting gift to you." That is love.

- God imposes norms. We shape our life according to that model. That involves our entire life.

This is the ultimate goal of listening: hearing becomes obedience, total submission to the Word. We must be ready to stake our life on the Word of God.

The Israelites in the desert, assembled by Moses at the foot of Sinai, understood this well (Exod 19). The Lord had spoken to them, setting before them the covenant code, and they responded: "All that the Lord has spoken we will do, and we will be obedient" (Exod 24:7). Acceptance of the Word is expressed in a commitment that affects all of life. From this flow all the essential realities of the Old Testament: the covenant, which is ratified at once by sacrificial blood, and the people of God who are born from that first assembly.

And when the divine plan reaches its climax, this obedient faith is revealed in all its mysterious breadth, height and depth. Christ gives the Father the perfect response he was looking for: the total surrender of himself to the God who speaks.[92] His very entrance into the world occurs under the sign of this surrender:

> When Christ came into the world, he said, "Sacrifices and offerings you have not desired, but a body you have prepared for me; in burnt offerings and sin offerings you have taken no pleasure. Then I said, 'See, I have come to do your will, O God' (in the scroll of the book it is written of me)" (Heb 10:5).

Coming into the world is the fundamental orientation of Christ's life. It has rightly been said that this is the reason for the

---

[92] See the beautiful chapters Bouyer devoted to showing the complexity of this response to the God who speaks: *La vie de la Liturgie* (*Lex Orandi,* 20) Paris 1956, ch. III: *Du qahal juif à l'Ecclesia chrétienne,* 39–55. *Eucaristia,* Italian tr., ed. LDC, Turin-Leumann 1969, ch. III, *Parola di Dio e "Berakah,"* 37–56.

incarnation. Christ enters the world precisely to do what is written in the scroll of the Book. There is found the plan marked out for him by the Father. He will do only that, and he will do it all. He will give those words their full meaning—with his life. And so he fulfills the Scriptures. His actions and attitudes are constantly modeled on them: "As it is written" or "So that what is written might be fulfilled." And that plan will be carried out to the final iota. His last word, "I thirst," will come from his lips "so that the scripture might be completely fulfilled" (John 19:28). Thus we can say that his whole life is contained in the divine plan found in the sacred Book, a book of formation in the fullest sense of the term. What is more, Christ appeals to it when he is proposing a norm: "How do you read?" Thus we are justified in speaking of a biblical way of life.

A biblical way of life

Christ's attitude is, of course, the norm. Tradition understood this at once, especially with regard to the "new scroll" brought us by the Gospel. The Gospel and all that prepared its way must be lived. Charles de Foucauld said that "we must shout it with our life." Even our understanding of it passes through experience, as Jerome said. It is understood only by those who live it.[93] True exegesis explains the Word precisely by fulfilling it. If philology with its study of the words is cut off from this vital experience, it will be a science but not true Christian exegesis.

The mystery of the Word reveals its secrets not from teachers' desks but in churches and in the lives of the saints. *In churches,* where in the presence of the assembly what is proclaimed in the Word becomes real in the sacrament. It reveals its meaning in the very act of being fulfilled. *In the lives of the saints,* who let themselves be formed by that Word. A saint is a living Word, a sacred page by which God speaks to the world; a Gospel that flows from within, filled with new realism, because it is written on a soul not with ink, but with the Spirit of Christ.

[93] Jerome, *Epist.* 127, 4 (PL 22, 1089).

Here is a chance to look in tradition for some typical examples to imitate. For St. Benedict, the Scripture texts become "instruments of good works" (Rule, ch. IV). The meaning of the term "instrument" could be discussed, but one thing is certain: the Scripture texts listed in the rest of that chapter are essentially norms of life. They are divine requests that await a response in acts. This creates a twofold orientation. On the one hand, the whole spiritual life is linked to the text of Scripture; on the other hand, exegesis of that text is totally directed toward life. Here is a typical example from the Middle Ages. Nilus of Rossano was known to his contemporaries as an exegete. The monks of Monte Cassino, eager for commentaries to use in their *lectio*, sent to him asking for a treatise. The answer they received is worth more than a treatise: "I explain all of Scripture with my life." He was a saint and could say that.

But again it is Gregory who offers the most striking testimony about the vital link that must exist between Scripture and life. Speaking for all of tradition, he sees the essential unity between the Bible, the life of the Church, and the life of the soul. If the Bible is the history of salvation, the life of a spiritual person is its continuation and marks, as it were, its full flowering. Thus mystical experience is in vital continuity with the Bible because it is part of the history narrated there. The same Spirit who is the source of inspiration and who set the divine plan in motion is at work in every soul, causing it to relive the stages, guiding it to salvation along the same paths. The Bible marks the historical path of every soul to God.

All this is part of the great "dispensation of the Holy Spirit who ordains all things wonderfully," which must be completed in each of the elect until the end.[94] Every Christian life stands in the middle of that tension between the "already" and the "not yet" which characterizes the present moment in the divine plan. It stands between the wonders of the past and the glorious final consummation. It is linked to the first by faith and to the second by hope. The life of the saints (and such is the life of every baptized person) is the living link

[94] Gregory, *Moral.*, XXXV, 15, 41 (PL 76, 772c).

between past and future. It is the integrating element in salvation history.[95]

Gregory's *Dialogues,* a model of medieval hagiography, are the most eloquent illustration of this. He wishes to complete Scripture by offering living examples of how its marvelous deeds are continued in that phase of the divine plan we call modern-day life. The life of the *homo Dei* is an existential response to the basic question: How does one live the Bible? That is why the stages of his or her life are associated with the stages of the divine plan. The result is a schema, modeled on the historical outline of the Bible, which a modern historian would regard as fictitious. And as far as a detailed reconstruction of the facts goes, it is; but it does reveal a fruitful concept of the spiritual life. The *homo Dei* sums up all the experiences of the Old and New Testaments: prophets, apostles, martyrs. The call is modeled on that of Adam in Eden or Abraham in Ur of Chaldea. The temptations resemble those in Eden or the desert; prayer recalls Jacob's struggle with the angel, which ends with a face-to-face (though furtive) vision of God. The entire ascetical journey is seen as the return to paradise from a distant country. Death (on the sixth day, in the case of St. Benedict) brings the "earthly week" to a close. This "week" is modeled on the first biblical week of creation and represents the true entrance into paradise by a shining path that leads toward the East. In this way the Bible becomes the standard measure of spiritual experience. From Exodus to the Canticle to the Gospel, it leads the elect to union with God.

---

[95] Ibid. n. 49: "Let us remain faithful to historical truth without depriving prophecy of what is yet to happen. If the good we recognize in the lives of the saints is not true, it is nothing; if it has no 'mystical meaning,' it is very little. Therefore, may the life of the good, described by the Holy Spirit, be for us a shining light through spiritual understanding; yet may a sense of history not turn away from faith. The more firm the soul's understanding, the more it is situated, as it were, in the middle: facing the future with hope and the past with faith" (PL 76, 779d). See B. Calati, *Spiritualità monastica, "Historia salutis,"* Rome 1959; Idem, *S. Gregorio Magno e la Bibbia. La vita spirituale come risposta e compimento della Parola ispirata,* in *Bibbia e spiritualità,* cit., 121–78; R. Manselli, *Gregorio Magno e la Bibbia,* in *La Bibbia nell'alto Medioevo,* Spoleto 1963, 67–101.

Franciscanism, although it moved in a spiritual climate that was different in many ways, inherited this fruitful concept. One day Francis entered a church with his first recruit, Lord Bernard. They opened the Gospel and read there three invitations from the Lord, all of them pointing in one direction: "Sell what you have. . . . Take nothing for your journey. . . . Deny yourself and take up your cross." Francis concluded his reading with these words: "That is the counsel which Christ gives us. So go and do perfectly what you have heard."[96] And he did this *without any commentary.*

The scene embodies Francis's attitude before the Gospel: profound reverence joined with childlike simplicity. Above all, he was firmly convinced that it is useless to know the sacred verses if this does not lead to action. The great Bonaventure was amazed at the "remarkable acumen" with which Francis probed the depths of Scripture, although he had no scientific training (he referred to himself as "unlettered"). Bonaventure gives us the key to the riddle: "Where the scholarship of the teacher stands outside, the affection of the lover entered within."[97] As a lover of Christ, he wishes to follow closely in his footsteps through the Gospel.

What emerges most clearly from tradition is this. The Bible is not only a book to read, to learn, to pray over—an interesting and moving story. It is essentially a story to be relived. It presents me with things I cannot contemplate passively, as if it were an interesting story but one that did not concern me. I must react; I must relive the religious experience contained in the text. "To understand Scripture we must stop acting like mere spectators."[98] This statement by a great contemporary

---

[96] *Little Flowers,* ch. II.

[97] Bonaventure, *Legenda maior,* XI, 1.

[98] K. Barth, *Dogmatique,* French tr., vol. I, t. II, p. 175 and 118. Barth expressed a similar idea in these words, which are from the preface to the first edition of his *Letter to the Romans:* "Paul, as a child of his age, addressed his contemporaries. It is, however, far more important that, as Prophet and Apostle of the Kingdom of God, he veritably speaks to all men of every age. The differences between then and now, there and here, no doubt require careful investigation and consideration. But the purpose

theologian reflects perfectly the orientation of all classical exegesis: "Let them not think that this was not said to us just because we were not there then."[99]

By means of the Word, the religious experience of the biblical characters, which it reflects, lives again in me. This is one of Gregory's characteristic ideas.[100] Thus we have the series: experience, text, experience. Here again, reading links one experience with another: the religious experience of a person today with the privileged experience of those whom God chose as instruments of God's saving plan.

The goal of committed reading is vital assimilation. This comes "through understanding of the heart and imitation of life."[101] The description left us by Cassian in *Conference X* is perhaps one of the most eloquent pages on the subject in Christian literature. The immediate context is the psalter; but since the psalter is a prayed summary of the entire divine dispensation, it can be applied to the whole Bible. Here is his description of the wonderful experience of one whose life is an embodiment of the Word:

---

of such investigation can only be to demonstrate that these differences are, in fact, purely trivial. The historical-critical method of Biblical investigation has its rightful place: it is concerned with the preparation of the intelligence—and this can never be superfluous. But, were I driven to choose between it and the venerable doctrine of Inspiration, I should without hesitation adopt the latter, which has a broader, deeper, more important justification. The doctrine of Inspiration is concerned with the labour of apprehending, without which no technical equipment, however complete, is of any use whatever. . . . *Nevertheless, my whole energy of interpreting has been expended in an endeavor to see through and beyond history into the spirit of the Bible, which is the Eternal Spirit.*" See K. Barth, *Römerbrief*, 1st ed., 1919, V (emphasis ours). [English tr. Edwyn C. Hoskyns].

[99] Augustine, *In Joann.* XXX, 7 (CCL 36, 292).

[100] Gregory, *In Ezech.* I, 10, 38: "In the life of the holy Fathers we recognize what we must understand in Sacred Scripture. For their action in their prophecies clarifies for us what is said in the pages of the two Testaments" (PL 76, 901).

[101] Godfrey of Admont, *De decem oneribus Isaiae*, ch. VIII (PL 174, 1196d).

The zeal of his soul makes him like a spiritual deer who feeds on the high mountains of the prophets and the apostles, that is, on their most high and most exalted teachings. Nourished by this food, which he continually eats, he penetrates so deeply into the thinking of the psalms that he sings them not as though they had been composed by the prophet but as if he himself had written them, as if this were his own private prayer uttered amid the deepest compunction of heart. Certainly he thinks of them as having been specially composed for him and he recognizes that what they express was made real not simply once upon a time in the person of the prophet but that now, every day, they are being fulfilled in himself.

Then indeed the Scriptures lie ever more clearly open to us. They are revealed, heart and sinew. Our experience not only brings us to know them but actually anticipates what they convey. The meaning of the words comes through to us not just by way of commentaries but by what we ourselves have gone through. Seized of the identical feelings in which the psalm was composed or sung we become, as it were, its author. We anticipate its idea instead of following it. We have a sense of it even before we make out the meaning of the words. The sacred words stir memories within us. . . . Instructed by our own experiences we are not really learning through hearsay but have a feeling for these sentiments as things that we have already seen. They are not like things confided to our capacity for remembrance but, rather, we bring them to birth in the depths of our hearts as if they were feelings naturally there and part of our being. We enter into their meaning not because of what we read but because of what we have experienced earlier.

And so our soul will arrive at that purity of prayer. . . .[102]

Bernard sums all this up in a simple expression when he says: "Listen attentively within, and you will learn through personal experience what is happening."[103] More recently, Claudel is even more concise: "They [the words] have ceased to be external; they have become ourselves."[104]

---

[102] Cassian, *Coll.* X, n. 11 (ed.cit., 92–93).
[103] Bernard, *De conv. ad clericos*, III, 4 (PL 182, 836c).
[104] *Paul Claudel interroge l'Apocalypse*, 305.

"Adhere totally to the text. . . ."

To reach this kind of total commitment in our lives, we must begin by committing ourselves totally in our reading. Here Bengel's golden rule, already cited, applies well: "Adhere totally to the text, and refer what it says to yourself."[105] Let us begin with the first half of this sentence.

All our vital energies must come into play: understanding and its ability to penetrate in order to "read within"; the will and its capacity for commitment; the heart and its ability to react affectively; the imagination and its unlimited creative power in order to reconstruct events. We could go on.[106] This need must be emphasized in a world such as ours, where inflation of the written word has conditioned us to read quickly and superficially. Our eyes skim rapidly over the page, and our thoughts glide over the realities expressed by the words like water that runs over a rock without soaking in. We need to rediscover that fuller reading whose secret the ancients knew, which is able to enter within. In the last chapter we will have a chance to verify this.

But it is not enough to say that this commitment involves all of one's psyche. The supernatural faculties also play a major

---

[105] Cited above in subsection 3: *Recollection*.

[106] The ancients involved the body itself, since they normally moved their lips when they read. Reading aloud in this way leads to a special kind of memorization. This lies behind that equally typical feature of reminiscence, in which one text spontaneously evokes a series of others based solely on verbal similarities (see J. Leclercq, *L'amour des lettres*, op.cit., 73–74). Although we moderns have reduced reading to a matter for the eyes alone, it is not so clear whether or not this is a step forward. Even psychological intuition, closely associated with the creative play of the imagination, finds a place in the reading of the ancients. The Cistercians were masters at this. They interpreted the feelings and psychological states of the characters in the Bible. Sometimes the exegete places himself in the scene and dialogues with them, even going so far as to regard them as friends. He wants to discover their human face, their innermost feelings, the inner drama. All this presupposes great simplicity of heart, but it is not an idle game. On the contrary: it shows how seriously the event was relived.

role. A Christian is more than a body and soul; there is also the Spirit of Christ. One of the densest paragraphs in *Dei Verbum* describes well the supernatural powers involved in our response to God who speaks and is revealed:

> "The obedience of faith" (see Rom 16:26; compare Rom 1:5, 2 Cor 10:5-6) must be our response to God who reveals. By faith one freely commits oneself entirely to God, making "the full submission of intellect and will to God who reveals," and willingly assenting to the revelation given by God. For this faith to be accorded we need the grace of God, anticipating it and assisting it, as well as the interior helps of the holy Spirit, who moves the heart and converts it to God, and opens the eyes of the mind and "makes it easy for all to accept and believe the truth." The same holy Spirit constantly perfects faith by his gifts, so that revelation may be more and more deeply understood.[107]

Note that the text centers around the Pauline expression "obedience of faith." All our commitment, all the divine power that assists us through the grace and gifts of the Holy Spirit, are contained in that basic attitude of faith expressed in obedience. And how is obedience understood? As an unconditional surrender to God who intervenes in my life by speaking. It is the submission of my whole being to God's Word in freedom and in love. It is an unlimited credit I open for God in my life in order that he might reign there. It is a "yes" proclaimed with my whole life.

Only total surrender of this kind can open the soul's gates. Then the Word of God "speeds on and triumphs" (2 Thess 3:1) in us, fills our heart, and gives a divine thrust to our entire life, raising it to God.[108]

"... and refer what it says to yourself"

Personalization follows total commitment. The whole text concerns me, addresses my life in all its aspects. It is directed

---

[107] DV 5.
[108] Ibid., 26.

at everything I am; it responds to my personal problems and my concrete needs. And although it presents me with the paradigms of an objective and universal religious experience, this experience, guided by God, is such that it contains the experience of each individual.[109]

This important aspect of *lectio* deserves closest attention. Each of us is a unique reality, absolutely original and irrepeatable: "The creative idea of God is never repeated."[110] Each person is a circle of pure solitude where God's free will is at work, "solitude to which an overpowering Presence draws near and invites us to an unbearable conversation: *The Master is here and calls you.*"[111] The divine Master addresses a personal and unique message to each of us, but it is transmitted through the universal message of the Bible, which is external and transcends us because it is addressed to all. "The public 'objective' revelation of God in history is also a revelation of his ways with each of us."[112]

Here, at the level of the Word, we glimpse the tension that exists at the human and Christian level between person and community, or between the baptized Christian and the Church. Every human being is unique and at the same time linked to all other human beings by a deeply shared life and destiny.[113] The Word is part of this situation. It speaks to all—to the entire Church—and at the same time it speaks to each of us in our most personal and irrepeatable situation. Our task is to let this universal message sink into the very fabric of our existence. Then the text is internalized and individualized.

---

[109] Gregory, *Moral.* XXIII, 34: "God does not respond to each of us individually, but he speaks so as to satisfy the demands of all. If we seek our personal problems in Scripture, we find them there. There is a response for everyone together, and the life of the one who has gone before becomes an example for the one who comes after."

[110] See J. Leclercq, *Saint Pierre Damien, ermite et homme d'Église*, Rome 1960, 7.

[111] Words of Cardinal Montini in a letter to the priests of Milan, Holy Thursday, 1958.

[112] C.H. Dodd, *La Bible aujourd'hui*, French tr., Ledoux 1957, 161.

[113] See R. Guardini's deep study of this tension in *Il senso della Chiesa*, Italian tr., Brescia 1960.

Classic tradition is once again our teacher. We have already seen that, for the ancients, the entire Bible is centered around Christ. Only his mystery can make the divine plan intelligible; but this mystery must be continued. This takes place on two levels: in the Church as a whole, which continues Christ in time, and in each soul, "a microcosm of the perfect Church" as Origen said.[114] There pulsates the life of the great Body of Christ scattered throughout the world.[115] "Everything that happens to the Church happens also to each individual Christian," said Pascal. The cell lives the life of the body; every Christian life is mystically fruitful in the Church.

It follows from this that everything in Scripture can be allegorized, that is, referred to the mystery of Christ and the Church which is one with him. Second, everything can be moralized, that is, applied to the individual (the ancients called this tropology). Thus we pass from the objective to the subjective.[116] The Bible is internalized, brought into the house of the soul, as one Cistercian says.[117] Each one welcomes it and appropriates it. What took place in Christ and what takes place in the Church is fulfilled in each one.[118] It is the final stage of the mystery which in a way finalizes all the others.[119]

There is a deep inner logic to the process of spiritual exegesis that goes from objective history to the subjective internal state of the individual. The biblical data are not diluted from their original concentration; on the contrary, they reveal their fruitfulness. What would be the use of all God has done if it did not affect the life of each one? Failure to recognize this continuity is to mutilate the objective fact of the mystery.[120] It is like preventing a tree from bearing fruit.[121] We all know that doctrine is dry

---

[114] Origen, *In Ex.*, hom. 9, n. 3–4 (PG 12, 363–69).

[115] See our article "Interpretazione cristiana e liturgica della Bibbia," 13ff, in *L' "oggi" della Parola di Dio nella Liturgia,* LDC 1969.

[116] See Adam Scot, *De trip. tab., ep.,* c. 7 (PL 198, 631).

[117] Henry of Marcy, *De per. civ. Dei.,* tr. 15 (PL 24, 278b).

[118] Origen, *In Ex.*, hom. 3, n. 2 (PG 12, 313).

[119] See L. Bouyer, *L'initiation chrétienne,* Paris 1958, 113–14.

[120] See H. de Lubac, op.cit., I, 557 and n. 7.

[121] Alan of Lille, *Elucid. in Cant.* (PL 210, 102cd).

unless it is expressed in life and holiness. We also know that
morality is impoverished when it is divorced from mystery. The
present moment in theology, which is committed to the integration of doctrine and life, can avail itself of the rediscovery of traditional exegetical views. We will have not only a renewed
theology, but even more a new flowering of holiness.[122]

The entire Christian tradition worked hard to achieve this
union between Bible and life.[123] Here are a few witnesses. We
know Augustine's cry: "Pay attention, brothers and sisters
. . . it is really speaking about you."[124] Then there is Gregory:
"We must read as if it were about us." And again: "What is
told as having taken place outwardly, we know how it is accomplished inwardly."[125]

"All Scripture was written for us."[126] We discern the truth of
God's Word more exactly when we search for ourselves in it.[127]

The Middle Ages continue this theme with infinite variations. The school of Citeaux stands out in particular, devoted
as it was to seeing the mystery precisely at its point of inser-
tion into one's inner life, to contemplating it through the filter
of personal experience.[128] For them the soul is "the temple of
God in which are celebrated the divine mysteries."[129] Frequent
use of terms such as "present," "every day," "today," "even
now," "always," "innermost," "within" expresses well the direction of their thought.[130] Everything is accomplished within.

[122] See J. Leclercq, *Teologia e preghiera*, in *La preghiera nella Bibbia e nella
tradizione patristica e monastica*, Rome 1964, 951–71.

[123] H. de Lubac, op.cit., I, 549–86.

[124] Augustine, *Serm.* 8, c. IX, n. 12 (PL 38, 72).

[125] Gregory, *Moral.*, I, 24, 33 (ed. *Sourc. chrét.*, 32, 162); II, 38, 63 (PL 75,
586c).

[126] Idem, *In Ezech.* II, 5, 3 (PL 76, 986b).

[127] Idem, *Moral.* XXVIII, 8, 19 (PL 76, 459c).

[128] See M. Magrassi, *La Bibbia nei chiostri da Cluny a Citeaux*, op.cit.,
227–39.

[129] Anonymous, *Tract. de interiore homine*, 1, 2: "The soul that possesses
God is the temple of God in which are celebrated the divine mysteries"
(PL 184, 509d).

[130] Henry of Marcy, *De per. civ. Dei*, tr. I: "According to the spiritual
meaning, the entire Old Testament concerning the future opens in ad-

This is exegesis at the service of spirituality. The committed nature of ancient *lectio* is based on it. If only we could rediscover its secret so as to share that fervor and that experience!

The soul, a microcosm of the Church

One might object that such a procedure poses two dangers: arbitrary subjectivism and individualism. We avoid the danger by making the moral sense pass through the mystical sense. In other words, before I apply the text to myself, I apply it to Christ and the Church. That which took place in him and continues in his mystical Body needs only to reverberate in me.[131] In that way, the experience created by the Word in me is modeled on that of Christ and is in harmony with that of all his members, even though in me it takes on nuances corresponding to my inner world. As was said of Bernard, it is "a Church experience"[132] in organic relationship with all its mysteries. It is a christocentric and ecclesial spirituality, and yet it becomes deeply personal.

Speaking of Gregory's *Commentary on Job,* Venerable Bede outlines his procedure in pellucid terms: "He wondrously taught how the book [of Job] was to be understood in the literal sense, how it was to be referred to the mysteries of Christ and the Church, and how it was to become life for all the faithful."[133] Christ, the Church, the individual: these are the steps through which the Word must pass.

Certain major themes permit me to pass from the abstract to the concrete. If I am considering the theme of Jerusalem, I will think of the dwelling place the divine architect wishes to build

---

vance, foretelling the threefold coming of Christ: in hiddenness and humility; in the sweet experience of the saints each day; in the expectation of his awesome appearing at the end of time" (PL 204, 259c).

[131] See the fruitfulness of this exegetical method in a modern commentary on the Psalms which uses it: S. Rinaudo, *I salmi preghiera di Cristo e della Chiesa*, Turin 1966.

[132] J. Mouroux, *Sur les critères de l'expérience spir. d'après les sermons sur le Cant. des Cant.*, in *Anal. Sacr. Ord. Cist.* 9 (1953) 256–57.

[133] Bede, *Historia Anglorum* II, 1 (ed. Plummer, Oxford 1956, 137).

in my heart. But I will see it as a reflection of that holy temple he builds every day in the Church.[134] If I am contemplating the birth of Christ, I will think of the interior coming that happens every day within my life. But I will experience its link to his humble and hidden birth in Bethlehem, to what happens every day in the Church and in the sacraments, a prelude to that glorious coming that will be revealed at the end of time.[135] If I am picking up the Canticle, I will feel the vibrations of God's personal love surrounding me; but I will situate this intimate relationship within the great mystery of the marriage between Christ and his Church. The bride is the Church, but at the same time I am the bride. One of Gregory's transitional formulas is significant: "What we have said of the Church in general, let us now see applied to each soul in particular."[136]

These are not two different interpretations. The one is situated within the other.[137] Here we have the teaching of the Cistercians, expressed in numerous treatises *De anima* and summed up by Bernard in the expression, "The affinity of the soul to the Word."[138] There is an affinity between the objective world of divine revelation and the Christian mystery and my subjective inner world, for the soul is made according to the image of God. These are not two dissimilar realities; they need to be integrated. The Bible helps me to know myself more deeply. Thus the close link between the inner search for Christ and the collective search of the City of God that takes place in salvation history. The story of the Bible is my story. To reach Christ I must travel the same path traveled by Israel, the same path the Church is traveling. And since the entire Bible is for me, as Gregory said, it must continue to be fulfilled in me. In some way it continues to be prophecy for me until it is fulfilled in my life.[139] While waiting, I must continue to "practice the

---

[134] See Origen, *In Ex.*, hom. 9, n. 3–4 (PG 12, 363–69).

[135] See Bernard, *Serm. in adv.* 4, 1 (PL 183, 47c); 5, 1 (50–51).

[136] Gregory, *In Cant.* 1, 5 (PL 79, 479b; compare 481c, 488b).

[137] See H. de Lubac, op.cit., I, 560–63.

[138] Bernard, *In Cant.*, serm. 81, n. 1 (PL 183, 1171b).

[139] See Philip of Harving, *De dignit.*, c. 6: "When he told them to act externally, he prophesied what would be fulfilled spiritually in us. And

Truth" according to St. Paul's happy phrase. Committed reading is the bridge over which biblical prophecy passes in order
to become *deed* in my life—every day. I should be able to say
of my *lectio* what Jesus said in the synagogue at Nazareth after
reading from the scroll of the prophet Isaiah: "Today this
scripture has been fullfilled in me" (Luke 4:21).

Mirror and sword

Two classical images complete the picture. They help us to
understand better the norm used by Bengel to sum up the tradition: "Refer what it says to yourself." The Word is a mirror
and a sword.

First of all, a mirror.[140] In what sense? In the obvious sense
that the Word reflects our image. It is the tool for a ruthless
diagnosis of our life. It strips bare our secret thoughts and reveals to us our heart.[141] It enables us to interpret our life, to
read in the book of experience.[142] Here in our inner world

---

so the real history of that time became a prophecy for us" (PL 203, 674d–
675a).

[140] The image is already sketched in the Letter of James (1:23). It is developed several times by St. Augustine, *In Ps.* 103, 1, 5 (PL 37, 1338), *In Ps.*
123, n. 3 (1641); even more by St. Gregory, *Moral.* II, 1 (PL 75, 553d). The
Middle Ages appropriated it and developed it in endlessly creative ways:
see R. Bradley, *Backgrounds of the Title Speculum in Mediaeval Literature*, in
Speculum (1954) 100–15; J. Leclercq, *La spiritualité de Pierre de Celle*, cit., 65:
La Bible miroir de l'âme. The council borrows it, but interprets it differently
than did the ancients: "This sacred tradition, then, and the sacred scripture of both Testaments, are like a mirror, in which the church, during its
pilgrim journey here on earth, contemplates God, from whom it receives
everything, until such time as it is brought to see him face to face as he really is" (DV 7). What is evoked here is the knowledge "through a mirror
in a dark manner" of which Paul speaks.

[141] Bernard, *De div.,* serm. 24, n. 2: "It is our food, sword, medicine,
security, rest, resurrection and final consummation. . . . The living and
active Word, which searches hearts and thoughts, examines the secrets of
our heart and judges them" (PL 183, 604a).

[142] Bernard, *De conv.,* III, 4: "Listen to the inner voice; use the eyes of
your heart, and you will learn by experience" (PL 182, 836c); *In Cant.,*

100 Lectio Divina: *Concrete Dispositions*

continues what John Scotus Eriugena said of the material world: sin has introduced agents of disorder that make it opaque to the light of God. The Word restores to our inner self its divine transparency; it gives us the key to decipher the book of experience.

But concretely, what is this key? It is the face of Christ reflected to us from each page of the Bible, like Veronica's veil. He is the image of the invisible God, but at the same time he is our image because we are called to reproduce in ourselves the features of his face. That is what happens when I read the Scriptures. I see reflected the face of Christ, and alongside his, my own. In other words, I see what I should be and what I am. Suddenly I realize what I am lacking in terms of conformity to the model. The diagnosis becomes sure and cutting: "There we come to know our good and our bad."[143] I have a valid standard to measure the consistency of my spiritual progress.[144] But above all, I feel a compelling desire to become what I should be. Thus I am inspired to imitate the divine model. The entire Bible is the book of the imitation of Christ. It reflects not only the face I was born with, as James says; it also reflects the face of my rebirth.

Alongside the symbol of the mirror is that of the sword which reinforces it. The Letter to the Hebrews had already said: "Indeed, the word of God is living and active, sharper than any two-edged sword, piercing until it divides soul from spirit, joints from marrow; it is able to judge the thoughts and intentions of the heart" (Heb 4:12). The image is particularly effective. The Word must wound. In other words, it must challenge false situations, give rise to second thoughts, create *metanoia*. If the Word grazes the outer layer of the soul without wounding our thoughts, heart and life, reading becomes formalism. The Word which proceeds from God's innermost life

---

serm. 3, n. 1: "Today the text we are to study is the book of our own experience. You must therefore turn your attention inwards, each one must take note of his own particular awareness of the things I am about to discuss" (PL 183, 794a).

[143] Gregory, loc.cit., in note 140.
[144] Idem, II, 1, 14 (PL 76, 945).

wishes to lay hold of ours, to reach the depths of our being, the "marrow." The prophets described this realistically: "Son of man, eat this scroll." Eating is the act that seals Ezekiel's vocation. Jeremiah, too, feels the Word like a burning fire shut up in his bones (20:9). It is like lava that explodes from a volcano and forcefully creates a channel: "I am weary holding it in, and I cannot."

A Word deeply suffered, it will pierce the hearts of others after passing through my own:

> I will speak, I will speak! May the sword of God's word pass through me to pierce the heart of my neighbor! I will speak, I will speak! May I understand the word of God, even if it is against me![145]

These are Gregory's words. They are echoed in a modern novel,[146] where a priest addresses a fellow priest in these words: "The Word of God is a red-hot iron! And you who teach it, you'd go picking it up with a pair of tongs lest you burn yourself? Wouldn't you grab hold of it instead with both hands? . . . I simply mean that when the Lord happens to draw from me some word for the good of souls, I know, because of the pain of it." Then, as Cardinal Bevilacqua said, I present to my brother or sister "a Word that comes from my blood and guts, from the subsoil of my creatureliness." That Word contains a piece of my soul and has that irresistible tendency to spread which is proper to all experience. Its ability to affect the life of someone else is in proportion to how much it has affected mine.

---

[145] Gregory, *In Ezech.*, XI, 1, 5 (PL 76, 907–8).
[146] Georges Bernanos, *The Diary of a Country Priest* [Tr. Pamela Morris, modified].

$\bumpeq$ 5 $\eqcirc$

Lectio Divina: Four Acts

It would be pointless to ask the ancients for concrete and detailed methods of reading, similar to those established by recent schools of spirituality for mental prayer. The ancients apparently distrusted methods that were too rigid, that bound the human mind to a series of well-defined attitudes. Perhaps they were afraid of extinguishing the spontaneous freedom of the children of God in dialogue with the Father. In real life, the attitudes demanded and evoked by the Word are simultaneous and intermingled. Our ancestors knew this and said so repeatedly.

Nevertheless, a series of acts can be established, at least logically speaking. It was not until Guigo II, prior of the Grande Chartreuse (d. 1188), that this was done in a systematic treatise.[1] All the elements in Guido's classification already exist in the preceding centuries. They are amply illustrated and fervently and enthusiastically lived. But no one thought to classify them. The ancients had no need for our kind of logic; the logic of experience was enough for them. But we cannot do without it, at least if we wish to provide an explanation. And so we will follow Guigo's outline, adding the most important data from earlier tradition. It is not our intention to exhume a

---

[1] Guigo II, *Scala claustralium, sive de modo orandi* (PL 184, 475–84). English tr. Edmund Colledge and James Walsh.

dead treatise, but with it we wish to discover again a living experience of the Word in its chief moments.

Prayed reading was traditionally described by an ascending series of terms: reading, reflection, study, meditation, prayer, contemplation (in Latin: *lectio, cogitatio, studium, meditatio, oratio, contemplatio*). Study and reflection are actually part of meditation. Thus Guigo retains four terms: reading, meditation, prayer, contemplation.

These four are rungs on an ascending ladder whose lower end rests upon the earth and whose top pierces the heavens.[2] An amazing trajectory, it begins with reading and ends in contemplation, which is a prelude to vision. Here is the first important point: all religious experience, until it erupts in mystical experience, is solidly linked to the Bible. Classical antiquity could imagine no other foundation for spirituality.

These four acts are intimately connected: "They are linked together, each one working also for the others."[3] They are stages in a single movement of the soul and are influenced by one another. Hugh of Mortagne expresses this concisely: "When I read I pray, and when I pray I contemplate."[4] Reading bears fruit only in contemplative prayer. And the latter must flow from reading in order to avoid becoming lost in vain fantasies or sentimentality.

But what are the four stages, and how are they related to each other? Guigo replies with an image: "Reading, as it were, puts food whole into the mouth, meditation chews it and breaks it up, prayer extracts its flavor, contemplation is the sweetness itself which gladdens and refreshes." Or again, without the image: "Reading works on the outside, meditation on the pith: prayer asks for what we long for, contemplation gives us delight in the sweetness which we have found."[5] The

---

[2] Ibid., loc.cit., (475cd).

[3] Ibid., c. 11 (481d).

[4] Ms. Lat. 3.589 of the Bibliothèque Nationale de Paris, cited in J. Leclercq, *La Liturgia e i paradossi cristiani*, cit., 279; see Smaragdus, *Comm. in Reg. S. Ben.*, ad cap. 4, n. 57: "Prayer must not be opposed to reading or vice versa."

[5] Guigo II, op.cit., c. 2 (476c); c. 10 (481c).

image of eating expresses well the overall goal: to take the word into ourselves in order to assimilate it. By means of the Word we are assimilated to God so that we might live by him. We illustrate briefly the individual phases.

Reading

The starting point is reading. With it I get ready to listen: God speaks to me.[6] It is the moment when, as Jerome would say, "I unfurl my sails to the Holy Spirit"[7] in whom I have the joy of hearing the Lord's true voice.

Full hearing requires *attentive* reading. Even before we reflect, we must listen and receive. In fact, the most important attitude before the God who speaks is openness. But this will not be complete unless we read with commitment, as described above.[8] The only thing we would add is a comment of Aldelm of Canterbury. Stressing the arduous nature of this commitment, he compares it to the work of bees gathering nectar from the flowers.[9]

Here we would like to underscore another requirement: contemplative calm. All haste is excluded. We moderns, when we read, are usually in a hurry. Our haste stems from curiosity and a thirst for novelty. We can see this in the avalanche of written words in which we are drowned, thanks to modern publishing. But this is deadly when dealing with a Word that holds the mystery of God. It prevents us from understanding, and above all, from assimilating. We cannot find what we are looking for. The *Imitation of Christ* had already observed this. Not in haste, it says, adding that curiosity which gives rise to haste is a major obstacle in the reading of Scripture.

In the prologue to his *Orationes sive meditationes,* St. Ambrose notes that "we should read them [the words] not in agitation, but in calm; not hurriedly, but slowly, a few at a time, pausing

---

[6] See chapter IV, d: *Dialogue.*
[7] Jerome, *In Ezech.*, praef. ad 1. XII (PL 25, 369d).
[8] See chapter 4, e: *Commitment.*
[9] Aldelm, *De virginitate,* 3–4 (*MGH Auct. ant.* XV–I, 1913, 231–32).

in attentive reflection. . . . Then the reader will experience
their ability to enkindle the ardor of prayer." This is essential
if reading is to lead to prayer. Prayer is one of those things that
cannot be done in a hurry. If we are in a hurry, all we can do is
read formulas.

The ancients were protected from this danger. The work involved in copying codices made them extremely precious. According to Jerome, the young St. Hilarion copied the codex of
the Gospels in his own hand.[10] In 735 St. Boniface had the letters of St. Peter copied to take with him on his apostolic jour-
neys. To the abbess Eadburga he recommends: "Set every
letter in gold . . . to honor and reverence the sacred Scriptures. . . ."[11] Who has not heard of the magnificent illuminated codices that resulted from this spirit? It not only testifies
to an infinite reverence for the sacred text; it is also the sign of
attentive and careful reading. No one wasted that much time
copying a text just to let it gather dust on the shelf. Books were
precious, and the ancient reader exploited them like a miser.
But the ease with which we moderns can obtain books has
accustomed us to reading badly. We must get to the bottom of
this habit. Even though the text is not printed in gold letters,
but with common ink on an ordinary sheet of paper, it is still
the same divine letter from heaven. Our eyes will not skim
rapidly over the page but will gaze peacefully at each word. In
an atmosphere of prayer and recollection, we will try to cross
its threshold in order to enter the mystery contained within.

In what order should we read the various books of the
Bible? It is hard to give definite and universally valid rules.
Much depends on each one's concrete situation. Still it is legitimate to think that the most fruitful method is the one followed by the Church in the liturgical cycle. It is the fruit of two
thousand years of experience guided by the Spirit. Private
reading should normally be coordinated with it.[12]

---

[10] Jerome, *Vita S. Hilarionis*, 35 (PL 23, 48).

[11] Boniface, *Epist.* 35 (ed. R. Rau, Darmstadt 1968, 114).

[12] The outlines for a distribution of the Bible readings put out by ABI
(Associazione Biblica Italiana) deserve a quick mention. Among the

This is not the place for a detailed explanation of the criteria followed in the new order of Sunday and weekday readings. It is enough to say that it is an adaptation of two different methods. For solemnities and major seasons of the liturgical year, selected pericopes are read that relate to the mystery celebrated. At other times the readings are semi-continuous: one book is read from beginning to end, more or less long pericopes being taken from it, obviously the most important. Both criteria are traditional.[13] Mostly traditional, too, is the assignment of a particular book to a particular period of the liturgical year. This has been adopted in line with the requirements of the three-year cycle for feasts and the first reading of the two-year cycle for weekdays. Traditional practice, with some appropriate integration, results in a schematic list more or less like this:

Protestants there are older and better known initiatives. For example, *Losung* ("Motto") suggests one verse of the Bible as a motto for every year, every month, and every day. Here is an example:

> *Jahreslosung* 1969: "For the word of the Lord is upright, and all his work is done in faithfulness" (Ps 33:4).

> *Monatspruch,* August 1969: "Why is it thought incredible by any of you that God raises the dead?" (Acts 26:8).

> *Losung* for August 18, Tenth Sunday after Trinity: "When I sit in darkness, the Lord will be a light to me" (Mic 7:8). "The light shines in the darkness, and the darkness did not overcome it" (John 1:5). Readings for the same day: Luke 19:41-48 and Ps 55:2-17.

On the cover of the booklet appear these words: "With *Losung* we know what we have and who we have. With *Losung* we know who has us: God. With *Losung* we have his Word for every day. Every day has its own question, and every day has its own answer. There are a great many questions and answers; we find them in the newspapers, too. But the real question and the only answer is found in the Word. . . . With *Losung* we have the words of him whose farewell message was: "I am with you all days." (ed. *Evangelische Brüder-Unität,* Herrnhut).

[13] See A. Baumstark, *Liturgie comparée,* 136ff; A. Chavasse, *Les plus anciens types du lectionnaire et de l'antiphonnaire romains de la Messe,* RB 62 (1952) 3–94.

1. Advent and Christmas Season: Isaiah, Infancy Gospels. Time after Epiphany: Pauline Epistles.
2. Sundays before Lent (formerly Septuagesima): Genesis (first stages in the mystery of redemption).
3. Lent: Exodus, the Passover, entry into the promised land.
4. Passion Time: Jeremiah, Deutero-Isaiah (Suffering Servant Songs), Gospel Passion accounts, Letter to the Hebrews (the Messiah's priestly sacrifice).
5. Easter Season: Acts of the Apostles (life of the early Church), Apocalypse (glory of the Son of Man), Letters of Peter (paschal liturgy and baptismal spirituality), Letters of John and James.
6. Time after Pentecost: the remaining historical, wisdom, and prophetic books.

The Gospels are distributed over the entire year because the mystery of Christ is coextensive with all of salvation history and the church year which relives it. They are the object of constant re-reading. The Gospel of John is traditionally assigned to Lent and Easter Time in nearly all liturgies. These directions do not pretend to cover the whole Bible every year. That would be impossible for most people. It would demand too fast a pace, to the detriment of deeper understanding which requires—we repeat—an atmosphere of contemplative calm. We merely wish to stress the continuity that should link liturgical hearing and personal reading. If one Advent is not enough to "ruminate" Isaiah, we will return to it the next year and pick up where we left off. What matters most is that our reading pass through that work of vital assimilation called *meditation*.

Meditation

In his treatise, Guigo describes it in these words: "When meditation busily applies itself to this work, it does not remain on the outside, is not detained by unimportant things, climbs higher, goes to the heart of the matter, examines each point thoroughly." It means patient analysis and deeper study. A normal and necessary continuation of reading, it presupposes that I am able to create space in my heart for the Word of God to ring out. And it leads to living assimilation, which transforms me into a "living library." Let us briefly illustrate these stages, beginning with that which is logically first.

First, we must create within our heart a flexible space of resonance,[14] so that the Word can penetrate its deepest parts and touch its innermost fibers. This demands the kind of recollection we feel the need for when something great and beautiful appears in our life. A poem demands that we pause at the end for silence. A musical theme that has moved us continues to echo, sweetly and insistently, within our soul. We feel the need to keep listening to this inner echo until it has permeated every fiber of our heart. The Word of God is much more demanding than a musical theme and much more profound.

God said to Ezekiel: "All my words that I shall speak to you receive in your heart and hear with your ears; then go to the exiles, to your people, and speak to them" (Ezek 3:10-11). *Receive them in your heart:* in that interior space made wider by faith and love, where they can touch the inner strings and set them vibrating. This divine touch releases grace and salvation for yourself and others. In the mystery of the Word, it is God whom you meet.

St. Augustine, using an untranslatable expression, calls this space "the mouth of the heart."[15] And with that he introduces an image that will later be very successful, even until the present: meditation is compared to the assimilation of food. The heart is the mouth in which the text is chewed—or as they prefer to say, ruminated. We ponder each word in order to grasp its full meaning, imprint it on our memory and taste its sweetness, find joy and nourishment for our soul: "The more the Word of God is chewed in the mouth, the more sweetly it is

---

[14] See L. Alonso Schökel, *La Parola ispirata*, Italian tr., Brescia 1967, 354–56.

[15] This expression found fortune in the Middle Ages: see, for example, the texts cited by J. Leclercq, *Un maître de la vie spirituelle, Jean de Fécamp*, cit., 99, n. 3.

savored in the heart."[16] Although this image no longer suits
our taste, we must admit that it is expressive and pertinent.
We smile when we read in one of Bernard's sermons this invitation to his monks: "Be pure ruminants." But they probably
did not smile. It was something very serious, which they regarded as the culmination of the contemplative ideal. It demanded constant hard work. But, observes one of them, in
spite of difficulties and darkness, it is worth persevering because at the end we receive the gift of enlightenment.[17]

Generations of medievals were faithful to this. St. Francis was
still among those who nourished his spirit in this school. Celano
says of him: "His memory substituted for books, for he did not
hear a thing once in vain, for his love meditated ["ruminated"]
on it with constant devotion."[18] He adds that Francis considered this way of reading more useful than wandering about
through thousands of treatises. Thus he especially recom-
mended it to his followers.[19] Bonaventure gives the reason:
"The words of Scripture must always be ruminated in order to
be tasted and applied with fervor to the soul." This is necessary if the food of the Word is to become part of the reader and
thus food for the soul.[20]

Guigo gives us a concrete example of slow rumination. He
takes the gospel verse, "Blessed are the pure in heart, for they
shall see God," and chews each word, starting with the most
important ones: *pure of heart*. External purity is not enough; we
must purify the inside. This is necessary if we are to climb the
mountain of the Lord and stand in his sanctuary (Ps 23:3-4). A
difficult task, to be sure, but God's creative activity is with us
and is capable of renewing us within: "Create a pure heart in
me, O God" (Ps 50:12). The reward is wonderful: *we shall see
God*. We shall see the face of the Lord as he is, wearing the robe
of immortality and crowned with the diadem which the Father

[16] Oger of Locedio, *Serm. de verbis dom. in coena*, IV, 1 (PL 184, 895b).
[17] Othloh of St. Emmeran, *De spir.*, 21 (PL 146, 218).
[18] Thomas of Celano, *Vita* II, n. 102.
[19] See *Determinationes quaestionum circa Regulum S. Francisci*, q. 3 (ed. Quaracchi VIII, 339).
[20] Bonaventure, *Coll. in Hex.* (ed. F. Delorme, Quaracchi 1934, 218).

bestowed on him on the day of his resurrection and glory. That vision will satisfy us forever: "I shall be filled when your glory appears" (Ps 16:15, Vulgate). Who but the blessed can measure the joy of this supreme blessedness?

Guigo interrupts his reflection: "Do you see . . . how great a fire has been kindled from a spark?" Yet I am only a beginner. The well is deep, and I have only learned how to draw up a few drops of water. But there is more; try it yourself.[21]

By the end of this work, the Bible becomes second nature. Jerome is describing an essential part of his experience when he says that everything he had absorbed through long study had become second nature to him, thanks to daily meditation on the Scriptures.[22] The Word is so deeply assimilated that it becomes part of us, molding our thoughts, feelings and life. And since to share in a word is to share in the one who speaks it, by identifying with the text the soul is identified with Christ. A spiritual person becomes a living library. Eventually such people no longer need to read from the book, for they can read within themselves. Athanasius says of Anthony that his memory took the place of the book.[23] Bernard constantly mentions the book of experience from which we must read in order to understand the Word.[24] This allows us to roam freely within the world of the Bible, as Jerome did: "He roamed through all the Scriptures with his thought and memory."[25]

Inner reading, which does not require a book, can be done at any time of the day, even during work, if this is performed in an atmosphere of silence. That is what Paula admired in the farmers around Bethlehem. Whether they were plowing, harvesting grain, or pruning their vineyards, the words of the

---

[21] Guigo, op.cit., c. 3 (477).

[22] Jerome, *Epist*. 127, 7 (PL 22, 1091).

[23] Athanasius, *Vita S. Antonii*, Bk I: "For he so listened to the reading that nothing of what was written escaped him, but he retained everything, and for the future his memory served him instead of books" (PG 26, 846a).

[24] Just as, conversely, we must meditate on the Word in order to interpret our experience; see Bernard, *In Ps. Qui habitat*, s. 7, n. 11 (PL 183, 206b).

[25] Jerome, *In Epist. ad Gal.*, III, 15 (PL 26, 364).

psalms, translated into song, rose spontaneously to their lips, expressing the joy that filled their simple hearts.[26] Pachomius's monks can sing a Scripture text while they are putting the bread in the oven or carrying home the baskets of fragrant loaves.[27] "To meditate on something from Scripture," even during the most mundane actions, is the leitmotif of his Rule.[28]

Why could we not repeat this wonderful experience? A proverb says, "The tongue ever turns to the aching tooth." This is what happens in the case of popular songs, is it not? Could not the psalms, which Christians sing over and over in the assembly, rise from the lips of farmers, artisans and laborers during their work? Would this not be normal, at least for consecrated religious? The texts return spontaneously to the lips of those who carry them in their heart and strive each day to fix them ever deeper. As they come to mind during the day, they are expressed in ejaculations, sometimes purely mental, sometimes formed by the lips in the language of the Bible. Often some unexpected illumination sheds new light on those words, and their meaning is seen more clearly than ever before. It is not the monotonous repetition of trite texts but the joyful discovery of a Word ever fresh and new.[29] What solidity and vigor it brings to our whole spiritual life!

Prayer

Meditative reading as we have described it leads spontaneously to prayer. In fact, it is prayer: "Reading, too, is prayer."[30]

[26] Idem, *Epist.* 46, 12 (PL 22, 491).

[27] Pachomius, *Regula,* 116.

[28] Idem, *Regula,* 142; *Regula,* 37.

[29] There is a significant anecdote from the desert Fathers in this regard. One monk knew fourteen books of the Bible by heart. But one day as he was on his way to the oratory, suddenly, as if by a flash of lightning, he was enlightened as to the meaning of one word. The impression was so strong that he could not utter a single verse during the Office. See *Verba seniorum* (PL 73, 930). See also C. Marmion, *Cristo ideale del monaco,* Italian tr., Padua 1948, 335.

[30] We read this statement in connection with St. Irenaeus of Marseilles; see Mabillon, *Acta SS. O.S.B.,* VI, 1, 611.

In any case, the two activities complement each other.[31] They are two moments in the mystical dialogue, harmoniously alternating.[32] The soul leaves its reading to run to God. William of St. Thierry calls this "meditative prayer": it springs from the heart at the touch of the divine Word. There is no easier or surer way to express ourselves to God. All we need to do is read, listen and ruminate. Then, having filled those words with all our thought, our love and our life, we repeat to God what he has said to us. The Word is not only the center of our listening; it is also the center of our response.

Pascal said that only God knows how to speak properly to God. The classical method, always found in the liturgy, is based on this conviction. The liturgy is essentially a Word returned to God. To return it, I must first receive it and assent to it: "To say yes is already to be saved," wrote St. Bernard.[33] The mind is attuned to the voice;[34] the human spirit joins in unison with the Spirit of God through his Word. I receive it from him as a grace, I make it my own, I taste it, I love it, I say my "Amen" with the saints in heaven. Then I give it back to him in an act of thanksgiving. All this is an act of recognition, an authentic eucharist.[35] It is the most authentic form of Christian prayer.

All we need to do is look at the liturgy, the Church at prayer. There the dialogue between God and God's people occurs in three stages:

1. Reading: God speaks.
2. Responsorial song: the people's response, a lyric moment of sung prayer. The Word descending into our hearts causes them to vibrate and creates an echo in song. That song is the exultant thanks of our whole being, rapt in contemplation of the mystery revealed to us by the Word. It is a

---

[31] See Defensor of Ligugé, *Liber scintillarum*, VII, 14 and 54 (*Sourc. chrét.* 77, 131, 141).

[32] Jerome, *Epist.* 107, 9: "Let reading follow prayer and prayer follow reading" (PL 22, 875).

[33] Bernard, *Liber de gr. et lib. arb.*, 1, 2 (PL 182, 1002).

[34] See St. Benedict, *Regula*, cap. 19; Vatican II, SC 90.

[35] See L. Bouyer, *Eucaristia*, op.cit., 37–47.

response in which we normally speak to God using God's own words: the psalms or scriptural canticles.

3. Silent personal prayer. The song tends to fade into silence. This is the most personal and meditative moment of the response, a free outpouring of the soul which has been personally touched by some of the words it has heard.

This is the method the Church uses to pray; it knows no other. It has meditated so long on the Bible that, when it wishes to speak to the Lord, it can only use the same words after it has made them its own. Mary, the model and "best part" of the Church also prayed this way. Her Magnificat is a patchwork of biblical texts. Verses from the Psalms and the Canticle of Hannah spontaneously rise to her lips, and she sends them to God in a joyful hymn of praise and thanksgiving.

Obviously, personal prayer must be modeled on that of the Church. Although a person-to-person dialogue will not have the sung response, the basic fact remains that a Christian who prays can only respond to God. In order to pray, we do not need to rack our brains, artificially evoking interior acts, thoughts or excessively refined affections. All we need to do is react in the presence of the text with free and spontaneous prayer. And when this spontaneous outpouring stops, we return to the text for fresh nourishment.

Too often prayer dies on our lips or takes refuge in mechanically repeated formulas. Or if we insist on pressing our inner faculties into service, it vacillates between dry reasoning and sentimental daydreaming. Lacking nourishment, it runs on empty. There is only one remedy for this: to nourish prayer with the rich deposit left in us by the Word, either read silently or heard live in the liturgical proclamation. There we find irresistible words that go directly to the heart of God. From there we can change the accents to express to God the various movements of our heart. And when spiritual dryness prevents us from doing anything else, it is enough to address to him the same words God has spoken to us, making certain that our mind and heart are in harmony with them. This will not be simple repetition because that word, having touched my life, is rich with new meaning.

If I hear the Word of Christ calling himself the way, the truth and the life, I will tell him that he is *my* way, the truth that enlightens *my* steps, the life that makes *me*, poor mortal that I am, a child of God. No longer will I wander about in a vacuum searching for elusive formulas. No longer am I ignorant of the way that leads to the sources of prayer; the Word of God shows it to me. Spontaneous and confident dialogue begins in the breath of the Spirit who animates me within.[36] The "sighs too deep for words" he places on my lips are those he placed on the lips of God's friends in the Old and New Testament. My prayer contains all the faith, hope and love that animated the people of the Bible in their long journey to Christ and that animates the Church on its pilgrimage to the Father's house. Picking up the Book, I fall on my knees, for it is the place and the means for encountering the living God.[37]

The Bible is, first, a manual of prayer. Only those who know how to read it, said Jerome, "know how to speak to the Spouse and have a taste for holy conversation." The ancients thought that "the words of God, of the saints, and of the liturgy, meditated and repeated unceasingly, had a sovereign power of withdrawing the soul from anxious self-consideration, in order to possess it completely and introduce it into the mystery of God and his Christ."[38] The council was right when it said that Scripture contains "a wonderful treasury of prayers"[39]—not only in the sense that it provides us with wonderful models, but in the broader sense that it nourishes the most authentic movements of Christian prayer. All Christian prayer, the highest forms of contemplation included, fits into this pattern of listening and response which is prayed reading.

---

[36] See Jerome, *Epist.* 130, 8: "Seek him whom your heart desires and speak to him confidently."

[37] Idem, *Epist.* 130, 15 (PL 22, 1119).

[38] P. Delatte, *Comm. à la Règle de Saint Benoît*, Paris 1948, 349.

[39] DV 15.

Contemplation

Contemplation is certainly the peak of this entire activity. It is not something superimposed from without but is like a delicious fruit that ripens on the tree of Bible reading. And it is a normal fruit—provided we do not understand the term to mean extraordinary mystical graces. There is, in fact, a form of contemplation available to all. It is a normal complement of the Christian life taken seriously.[40]

To contemplate means to enter into a relationship of faith and love with the God of truth and life, who has revealed his face to us in Christ. That face is revealed to us on every page of the Bible. All we need to do is *look:* open ourselves to the light and desire that it shine in us. Look *with admiration:* ecstasy in the presence of the good and the beautiful. *With a child's eyes,* that is, with a clear gaze that opens on reality as after a dream, delights in it, is amazed, and sees its perennial newness. *In silence:* the atmosphere in which the most important communication and the deepest insights occur.

On the natural plane, it is the attitude of a poet; on the spiritual plane, that of a contemplative. The Bible, as Claudel said, is "the book of admiration and contemplation," for it opens to the eyes of faith the poem of "God's wonderful works." These are the deeds that reveal God's holiness in act and culminate in the mystery of Christ. Standing before this awesomely beautiful picture, what else can we do but contemplate? A simple and spontaneous act, it is full of religious connotations: awe, admiration, thanksgiving, adoration, song, confession, praise. Prayer becomes a hymn of admiration in which the soul expresses in the language of praise the sweetness of what it has contemplated in him: "We feel delight when we speak of you, listen to you . . . discuss with others about you."[41] The ancients called this "theology." It is the attitude of the Church

[40] See the beautiful lecture by R. Voillaume, *La contemplazione nella Chiesa contemporanea,* published in three installments in *L'Osservatore Romano,* 6, 7–8, and 9 July 1969.

[41] These words are from the *Confessio theologica* of John of Fecamp (ed. J. P. Bonnes - J. Leclercq, *Un maître de la vie spirituelle,* op.cit., 182).

in its celebrations: "Hail, O Cross, our only hope . . . O night truly blessed . . . How boundless your merciful love!" And not only before the mystery of Christ, but also before the saints in whom his wonders are revealed: "Behold a man whom words cannot describe. . . ."[42]

From this arises a spirituality we could describe as "objective." Completely centered on the great object, it is less interested in analyzing the inner states of the praying subject, the rooms of the interior castle. What matters is to hear him, gaze on him and remain under his great light.[43] As long as prayer remains close to the Bible, it preserves this tone; when the sense of the Bible tends to be dimmed, subjectivism reigns. History is clear in this regard. Fortunately the Church's prayer, the liturgy, has kept intact this atmosphere of traditional prayer down through the ages. Now that it is being relived, we are joyfully rediscovering its treasures. Liturgical spirituality is defined by its close links to the Bible. The spirituality of each person will be liturgical to the extent that it has the Bible as its foundation.

But when the ancients speak of contemplation, they are not thinking only of the basic attitude described above. They are thinking of a particularly rich religious experience, a fruition that seems to anticipate the joy of heaven. The books are filled with striking descriptions. It is an experience of Sacred Scripture that kindles a fire in the soul and "suspends" it from heaven and its joys.[44] It is a state in which the soul, "suspended by the thread of contemplation, is lifted above the weight of human frailty."[45] Or, "when the spirit is warm, when the heart is white-hot, when fire is bursting the lover's bones."[46] It is a flight in which the soul, going beyond the words of the text, enters into union with the divine Word in anticipation of heaven.[47] Note the constant link between sight

[42] From the Office for St. Martin of Tours.

[43] This expression is from the famous "elevation" by Sister Elizabeth of the Trinity, cited in the previous chapter.

[44] Gregory, *In Ezech.*, 1, 8 (PL 76, 844d).

[45] Peter of Celle, *Serm.*, 12 (PL 202, 671b).

[46] Idem, *De disciplina claustrali*, 15 (PL 202, 1119b).

[47] See Gregory, *In Ezech.*, 1, 3 (PL 76, 806–12).

and the theme of "suspension," in which contemplation represents the thread.

Sometimes the descriptions become longer and more urgent. We sense that the author is stammering, that words are powerless to describe such a rich experience. Yet every phrase is a powerful brush stroke. Here is John of Fecamp's description:

> There are many kinds of contemplation, O Christ, by which devout souls find their joy and progress. But none brings me such joy as that in which my soul, laying aside all other things, raises its eyes to you, my only God, in a simple gaze that comes from a pure heart. What peace, what rest, what joy to the soul that is turned toward you! When my soul is longing to see God, when it is meditating and proclaiming your glory according to its ability, then the very burden of the flesh is lightened, violent thoughts are calmed, the weight of our mortality and misery does not dull our faculties as it usually does. All becomes quiet and calm. The heart burns with love. . . . The soul overflows with joy, the memory with strength, the intellect with light. And the whole mind, ardently longing to see your beauty, is caught up in the love of invisible things.[48]

The experience behind a text such as this borders on ecstasy. Even closer, perhaps, is this other very rich medieval text:

> As the human soul climbs the rungs to the summit of sure contemplation, it anagogically contemplates the secrets of heaven by piously searching the divine word. . . . At that point the human soul is trembling and shaking. . . . The awestruck soul is rapt in contemplation; anxious, it is filled with wonder. Whereas before it spoke; now it is utterly speechless. Formerly enriched by its poverty, now it is impoverished by its riches. Amazingly, it becomes weak as it advances, but then in its weakness it advances further. . . .[49]

Once we have reached this point, we can go no higher; we are at the threshold of vision. We are at the final stage of the jour-

---

[48] John of Fécamp, *Confessio theologica*, loc.cit.
[49] Garnerius of Rochefort, *Serm.*, 23 (PL 205, 730bc).

ney that begins with *lectio* and ends with astonishing intimacy with God. There is nothing left except that contemplation which fills the eternal day—beyond veils, words, and symbols.

Now we can fully understand the ancients' enthusiasm for Bible reading. Perhaps we can make our own the cry of Gregory: "How wondrous is the depth of God's words. What joy to fix our gaze there and penetrate its secrets with grace as our guide."[50]

---

[50] Gregory, *In Ezech.*, V, 1, 1 (PL 76, 821).

⊷ 6 ⊶

The Ancient "Conference" and the Modern Review of Life

At this point it is natural to compare traditional *lectio* with more original contemporary forms of reflection on the Word. One thing is certain. Whereas *lectio divina* is an exercise that involves individual prayer, modern forms take the shape of prayer groups that meet for common reflection.

But the ancients, too, knew how to read in groups. Besides *lectio* there was the conference (*collatio* in Latin). We have documentation even if we cannot always describe its actual development. Pachomius envisions fraternal collaboration in the act of rumination: "Let them ruminate together. . . ."[1] Isidore of Seville, attentive as always to the pedagogical aspect of the spiritual life, devotes a chapter to the conference. From it emerge the principles on which it is based.[2] He begins by saying that it is superior to individual reading: "It is better to confer together than to read." He goes on to describe the fundamental attitude that must animate it: receptive openness to the others. By adding together the lights and experiences of each one, we come to a deeper understanding of the Word. The questions, answers and objections provoke a more lively search, and then everything becomes clearer. Next he points

[1] Pachomius, *Regula* 122.
[2] Isidore of Seville, *Sent.* III, 14: *De collatione* (PL 83, 688–89).

121

out the two greatest dangers in such a group activity. The first is debate, which proceeds not from love of truth but from a desire to assert ourselves and our own ideas. Rooted in pride, it causes division and opposition and prevents access to the light. The second is pedantic hairsplitting, a form of erudite investigation and skill in dialectic that delights in subtle questions of detail. It blocks the way to a savory and vital understanding.

In short, what we are concerned with is a friendly and fraternal conversation in which ideas and experiences are shared. Individual reminiscenses are combined in the reading of Bible texts that illumine each other. In the same spirit, opinions are peacefully compared. There is, of course, someone to guide the discussion and prudently keep track of the threads. In monasteries, this is usually the abbot, but it can also be a brother especially versed in the sacred sciences, such as Bede or Rabanus Maurus.[3] All this is the normal continuation of personal *lectio*. What was received there is made available to all. Some give, some receive, and everyone comes away spiritually richer. This give-and-take depends on the amount of treasure acquired by each one in personal reading. But each one leaves the conference inspired by the contribution of the others.

Commentaries on the Rule of St. Benedict, such as that of Aldemar, show that common reflection of this kind must have been practiced in many communities.[4] One hopes they followed the wise directions of Isidore, later repeated by Defensor of Ligugé.[5] We cannot exclude the possibility that some medieval commentaries might have come from this, even though they bear the clear stamp of their editor.

We must admit that today's experiments, from Bible groups to the Focolare "Words of Life," are much closer to a monastic conference than to a scholastic disputation. The latter, which gained the upper hand in the thirteenth century, was decidedly aimed at creating an objective and detached science.

---

[3] Candidus, *Vita S. Eigilis*, c. 23 (PL 105, 399a).

[4] See J. Mattoso, *A "lectio divine" nos autores monásticos da alta Idade Média*, in *Studia monastica* 9 (1967) 185; H. de Lubac, op.cit., I, 85–94.

[5] See *Liber scintillarum*, c. 81, n. 38–40 (*Sourc. chrét.* 86, 316).

Today the word is leaving the walls of the classroom to become once more a Word of life for all Christians and their more active groups. It seems important, then, to re-create the spiritual atmosphere of that "sharing," with the necessary modifications to adapt it to our different mindset. Essentially it included the many values we have seen in *lectio divina*—only there they were lived in common. Monks dialogued with each other in order to arrive together at conversation with God.

As for the method of reflection that has done well in recent years and is known as the review of life, a comparison with *lectio divina* would be fruitful. This deserves a full study, but here we can give only a sketch.

The two methods seem to us strictly complementary. We can summarize as follows. *Lectio* begins with the Word and ends with life, in which it must be embodied. The review of life begins with a concrete event and ends with the divine Word that sheds light on its meaning for committed Christians. As we can see, the methods move between the same poles and involve essentially the same values. But they follow a reverse process, and this has a real pedagogical import.

When all is said and done, the review of life[6] is based on the profound faith insight that every event is a sign of God's presence in the world. It belongs to the story of the coming of the kingdom, since God is mysteriously at work there. But that is not immediately evident. The event, like the Word, is also a sign; it is a gospel opened to the right page. But we must learn to read within and discern its spiritual riches. The laws of the divine plan are always the same:

> The pattern of this revelation unfolds through deeds and words which are intrinsically connected: the works performed by God in the history of salvation (is it not ours as well?) show forth and confirm the doctrine and realities signified by the words; the words, for their part, proclaim the works and bring to light the mystery they contain.[7]

---

[6] See. J. Bonduelle, *La révision de vie, situation actuelle*, Paris 1964; Una équipe di figli della carità, *Revisione di vita per sacerdoti. Ricerche e testimonianze*, Italian tr., Bologna 1968.

[7] DV 2.

Clarifying the mystery of these works is precisely the task of the review of life. It realizes clearly that the key to their interpretation is found only in the gospel word. Here we are no longer speaking of God's great works in the Bible but of his interventions now in the fabric of our daily life. The point is this: *lectio* begins with a text, the review of life begins with an event. But they are complementary; both are the Word of God. Only in faith can I be open to the God who speaks; likewise, only with the eyes of faith can I discern the presence of God in an event. There is more. Just as the Word addresses me personally and wishes to take hold of my life, so too in an event: I am involved and committed. I feel as though I am inside it, and I ask myself how God is speaking to me through it. The two basic questions asked by the models are these. How is the presence of God revealed in this event? What is the Lord inviting me to do through it? We see that once again it is a matter of a listening attitude.

We have been speaking in the first person singular. Although this is appropriate for *lectio*, it is less so for the review of life. There the subject is the group as such: not "I" but "we." It is the moment when we live our faith vision together. But obviously we cannot contribute to a group review of life if we are not already used to engaging in a personal face-to-face with the Lord who reveals himself in events. Personal prayer and reflection prepare us for group work. The same relationship exists between these two terms as between *lectio* and the monastic conference.

What is new and original here is the choice of starting point. Modern people experience themselves first of all as "situated." Their greatest interest is the *Sitz im Leben*. No one can fail to see the pedagogical advantage of this connection with real life. The more intensely an event has been lived, the greater the connection. Thus the emotional intensity of an experience is made to serve faith and prayer. Everything tends toward the final goal: encounter with the Lord and dialogue with him, in order to work together for his coming in souls and in society.

The traditional method was born in a contemplative setting. Obviously, its starting point is direct experience of God. The modern method was born in a setting of lay people actively committed to a Christian presence in society.[8] Equally obvious, its starting point is a human experience in which the Lord's presence is incarnated.

But everyone can see how much the two methods need each other and the advantages that could come from their integration. We will need to be wise like the master of the household in the Gospel "who brings out of his treasure what is new and what is old": the age-old wisdom of the Church.

Conclusion

Gregory has played something of the role of protagonist in these pages. We would like to conclude by letting him speak once more. Among his letters is one addressed to Theodore, the emperor's physician. It is a jewel and worth re-reading today—not as a sixth-century document, but as a message from the great Pope to each of us at this rich and troubled moment in Church history, not unlike that in which he lived. Here is its main part:

> Since one who loves more risks more, I must reprimand my most illustrious son Theodore. He has received from the most holy Trinity the gifts of intelligence, well-being, mercy and charity. But they are forever being stifled by profane questions, by constant comings and goings. Thus he neglects to read the words of his Redeemer each day. What is Scripture if not a letter from almighty God to his creature? If Your Excellency lived somewhere else and received mail from an earthly monarch, he

---

[8] We know that the first ones to practice it were Catholic Action groups, especially the Young Christian Workers who were inspired by the late Cardinal Cardijn. Then it was adopted by the Sons of Charity, whose constitutions contain this paragraph: "Faithful to the teaching of Christ, the review of life is simply the discovery of the mystery of salvation fulfilled in secular events. It presupposes an acquired habit of attending to God's action in these events. It leads them to question their ways of thinking, judging and acting. In that way it becomes a genuine movement toward the Lord, a peak moment, experienced in common, in their religious and apostolic life."

would have no peace, he would not rest, he would not shut his eyes until he had learned the contents of that letter. The king of heaven, the Lord of men and angels, has written you a letter that you might live, and yet, illustrious son, you neglect to read it with ardent love. Strive therefore, I beg you, to meditate each day on the words of your Creator. Learn to know the heart of God in the words of God. Thus you will long for the things of heaven with greater desire, and your soul will be more eager for the joys that are invisible. . . . May the Spirit fill your soul with his presence, and in filling it make it more free.[9]

If each of us could feel that this appeal was addressed personally to us, if we could read the "divine letter" from our Creator in the same spirit, better days would lie in store for the Church—in its liturgy, its preaching and its spiritual life.

---

[9] Gregory, *Epist.* IV, 31 (PL 77, 706ab).